Put the

HEART

Back in Your
Community

Unifying Diverse Interests Around a Central Theme

LISA BROCHU | TIM MERRIMAN, PH.D.

heartfelt
PUBLICATIONS

Heartfelt Publications
Kealakekua, Hawaii
©2011
ISBN 978–0–9793933–1–0

Contents

1 **Sense of Place** *1*

Having HEART on a Large Scale—Curitiba, Brazil *8*

Sustainable Seattle *14*

Revitalization of Old Town Fort Collins—Colorado, USA *20*

2 **Holistic** *23*

Photo Essay: Paris, France *34*

Mto wa Mbu —Tanzania *36*

Photo Essay: Bar Harbor, Maine, USA *38*

Kansas Wetlands & Wildlife National Scenic Byway—Kansas, USA *40*

3 **Engaging** *45*

The Kohala Center—Hawai'i, USA *50*

GreenTown: Creating Opportunities from Adversity *54*

Photo Essay: Bath, United Kingdom *56*

Photo Essay: Monterey, California, USA *58*

4 **Appropriate** *61*

Cantera—Puerto Rico, USA *66*

Photo Essay: Washington, Arkansas, USA *72*

Photo Essay: Tuscany, Italy *74*

Working Together on a Growing Dream—Pueblo, Colorado, USA *76*

5 **Rewarding** *81*

6 **Thematic** *85*

The Heart of Santa Clara La Laguna—Guatemala *92*

Photo Essay: Mystic, Connecticut, USA *98*

7 **Creating Your Own Community Experience Plan** *101*

Photo Essay: Whitehall, Montana, USA *110*

Semai Communities—Malaysia *112*

8 **Resources for Staying HEART Healthy** *129*

Acknowledgements

Writing this book allowed us a unique opportunity to collaborate with colleagues and friends around the world. We wish to acknowledge and thank the following people who are helping create communities with heart all over the globe and who thoughtfully contributed to this effort: Paul Caputo masterfully did the layout and design and helped acquire needed photos. Dan Shilling and the ideas in his book on *Civic Tourism* stimulated many thoughtful discussions as we refined our own thought process. Cris Collier, author of one of our case studies, continues to be an inspiration and role model for excellence in collaborative communication. Chris Mayer's work in Guatemala, Panama, and other Latin American countries truly exemplifies the notion of leading a process with both your heart and head. Daniel Wallach and Catherine Hart were kind enough to review and improve our story about Greensburg, Kansas. Rick Price of Experience Plus introduced us to the unique landscapes of Tuscany and Val d'Orcia in Italy. Dick Mills of World Discovery Safaris introduced us to the good work of the people in the community of Mto wa Mbu in Tanzania. Our well-trained guides there showed exceptional thoughtfulness with our group that included diversity ranging from our teenaged grandson to Lisa's octogenarian mother and multiple nationalities. Fernando Silva and Eliezer Nieves showed us a Puerto Rico we had never seen and we deeply appreciate their heartfelt commitment to the Cantera community in San Juan. Masa Shintani has become a treasured friend whose dedication to being a positive influence in the world inspires, challenges, and humbles us. His influence has taken us to Japan and Malaysia where our experiences in Shibakawa, Kyoto, and Orang Asli villages have forever touched our lives. We also wish to thank I.S. Shanmugaraj and the outstanding young men and women of the Malaysian Nature Society for guiding us and introducing us to the kindness of the people in the villages of the Semai people.

In most cases, we have firsthand knowledge and experience with the communities represented in case studies and our observations are based on those experiences and our personal opinions of them. We apologize if you find anything in error but promise to correct anything that is less than accurate in future editions, if you will contact us by email and let us know. We are also interested in finding new case studies for the next edition of this book, so please feel free to share any examples you would like to see represented. We anticipate that this book will continue to be revised and improved as we see more communities begin to develop their own Community Experience Plans.

1 Sense of Place

What Defines a Community?

The dictionary gives several definitions for the word "community." A community can be any group of people who share a common interest. It can also be all the people and infrastructure they require in a particular area or physical location such as a village, city or town. Communities are really a matter of scale – the international community, for example, is a collective term for all the nations of the world. A forest community comprises all the living and nonliving things that make up that ecosystem bounded by the forest edges. For the purposes of this book, *a community is the built, social, and natural environments that comprise a defined location where people live, work, and play together.*

> A community is the built, social, and natural environments that comprise a defined location where people live, work, and play together.

The ideas and processes suggested in this book can be applied to a community of any size, from villages of fewer than 100 people to small towns with populations under 5000 individuals to sprawling cities or regions with populations of millions. Expanding or contracting the scale as necessary will require examination of the individual situation with appropriate adjustments made on a case by case basis. For example, a scenic byway would require looking at the collective experiences that create a unique regional community rather than isolating any one community or site along the byway. The important thing to remember is that a true community is one in which people are willing to work together toward a common good, framed by common core values.

How do communities establish core values?

The U.S. National Park Service describes core values as those "which form the foundation on which we perform work and conduct ourselves." They set boundaries for behavior and identify what we stand for by defining beliefs. They are not about strategies, tactics and operations. They are not so much rules as the belief system from which rules are derived. The U.S. Constitution begins with "We hold these truths to be self-evident, that all men are created equal . . . " That is a core value for the United States of America.

Communities evolve with unique cultural heritages and values that underpin the way people behave and live. Often those values go unstated, but in fact, they define the lifestyles of the community to some degree. The humorous and somewhat naughty tagline, "What happens in Vegas, stays in Vegas," is, in effect, a value statement. Adults sometimes feel they can do things in Vegas they would prefer not be known back at the office or hometown so the value is strangely comforting to those who go there to play in whatever manner.

> A true community is one in which people are willing to work together toward a common good, framed by common core values.

Ask yourself what you value about your lifestyle. What makes your community a wonderful place to live? When someone asks about your hometown, what are the consistent descriptions you share? If your children, families and schools share a common set of core values and deliver consistent messages about the

The spring Plum Festival in Kyoto, Japan, attracts visitors from all over the world to enjoy blossoming trees, street markets and traditional tea ceremonies. Vintage and modern kimonos can be found among the many temporary shops.

community, you build harmony. This harmony is the heartbeat of a community, the common culture formed from common beliefs, values, and behaviors. You can create or maintain a healthy heart in the community or you can even bring back the heart to an ailing community, but it requires involvement at all levels – young and old, powerful and helpless, governmental and private, rich and poor.

Identifying core values among community stakeholders through some combination of discussions, workshops, surveys, and facilitated sessions assists everyone in stating what they value and want to protect. If a community believes safety for children to play outside and a lifestyle of neighbors visiting on sidewalks and from porch to porch are important, that belief can be captured in a value statement such as, "We value safe neighborhoods that promote friendship and mutual support." If a community wants to expand but has concerns about long-term sustainability, the core value statement might be "we believe in thoughtfully planned growth through development of sustainable opportunities." These value or belief statements are not goals, but they do suggest goals that can then lead to identification of specific objectives for maintaining the community's sense of place.

What is sense of place?

When you think of New Orleans, you can't help but hear the sweet sounds of jazz in your mind. You can almost smell and taste the food - rich and spicy. Mardi Gras beads and masks can be found for sale throughout the year. In the French Quarter, the evening is just getting started at midnight, reinforcing the town's motto of *laissez les bon temps rouler* (let the good times roll). New Orleans has a distinct sense of place, something that makes it unique among other places in the world. It's so unique that even the battering of Hurricane Katrina in 2005 could not kill the spirit of this indomitable city as residents and tourists return to business as usual.

> Harmony is the heartbeat of a community, the common culture formed from common beliefs, values, and behaviors.

In the heart of Tuscany, residents walk medieval streets on paving stones older than the oldest homes in most American cities. They gather in the town piazza to enjoy music, eat bruschetta and drink fine wines in an outdoor café. Here, you can stop to drink espresso with your gelato at a coffee bar as you stroll to your home, enveloped in the fragrance of blooming vines and flower boxes. Tuscany offers a multi-sensory experience, charming in every way, justifying its well-founded romantic reputation. Locals brag about the fresh vegetables in every dish, the great wines produced in the hundreds of vineyards in the area, and the aromatic cheeses made in countryside cottages. The region has a rich sense of place, uniquely its own. If you're a visitor, you'll be planning your next visit before you've even left and imagining who will come with you, for the richness of Tuscany must be shared.

This planet has thousands of charming landscapes, villages, towns, and regions. But many of them are changing rapidly. What's at the heart of your community? Is it the original downtown with thriving local businesses or is it a shopping center with the same brand name chain stores that can be found in the next community down the road and the one after that? How do people

Street musicians in New Orleans add a recurring note to the enduring identity of this city.

San Quirico residents in the Tuscany Province of Italy gather along the narrow streets in the afternoon to chat among friends.

know they've arrived in your corner of the world? Or maybe the better question is, do they? If someone were to ask what makes your city special, what would the answer be? What makes you want to live there?

With the advent of successful chain businesses in thousands of communities, the generification of America and many other countries seems inevitable, impossible to resist in the face of growth and development. These wonders of mass-produced commerce sometimes pull the heart right out of a community, trading its charm and authenticity for the convenience of franchised business before anyone notices what's happened.

The timeless spell of Tuscany lives today in its small villages. In the shadow of Pitigliano's medieval walls, people sit in piazzas talking to friends as they've done for ages. Signs of franchise creep are missing and yet not missed. Somehow, international chains serving up coffee or chicken have not been placed among the beautiful buildings and landscapes of Tuscany. Yet, Tuscany enjoys thriving communities and a rich heritage tourism economy based on "agriturismo" or agricultural tourism. More than 600 of the small farms, vineyards and olive growers have converted or built buildings to provide services for bed and breakfast guests. Toscaneros have hung on to the heart of their communities by living and sharing the Tuscan lifestyle, with full understanding of the unique values that create the richness of this region. Certainly, Tuscany has thousands of years of history to help weave its magical tapestry, but even communities that are only centuries or decades old can do the same thing.

In Mountain View, Arkansas, old time music fills the town square in the evenings. At Jimmy Driftwood's barn, everyone from kids just getting started on guitar or fiddle to professional musicians play live on stage. The show is free and there are rocking chairs, straw bales and church pews to accommodate the audience, made up largely of locals. The spirit of Jimmy Driftwood, a songwriter with enduring country music credits including *The Battle of New Orleans* and *Tennessee Stud*, lives on as each generation passes its love for mountain music to the next one. Local cafés serve as eating establishments and gathering spots where local, regional, national, and global issues are discussed. Menus are filled with local specialties: biscuits and gravy for breakfast, deep-fried catfish with hushpuppies or pulled pork and fried okra for dinner. The Ozark Folk Center, run by Arkansas State Parks, is an integral part of this community. The center includes several performance venues and music festivals throughout the spring, summer and fall. Artisans demonstrate and sell Ozark crafts, making mountain dulcimers, wooden toys, and household items. Visitors to Mountain View immediately get a sense that music and the historic mountain culture is an important part of this place even today.

The heart of a community, its sense of place, is not usually City Hall, the hospital or even the schools, though they may certainly be part of it. A community's heart beats in the something special that makes it a desirable place to live, and that visitors describe to their friends when they return home. It can be enhanced by architecture, landscape, and activities but these tangible things are merely reflections of the location, not the intangible atmosphere created by its unique natural, social, and historical fabric. In short, no one thing defines sense of place – it is a combination of factors. Architectural historians call it genus loci, but no matter what term you use, the point is this: When it's there, it's pervasive and palpable, and when it's not, it leaves a gaping hole that drains the vitality from a community and paves the way for chain businesses to make it the same as anywhere else.

> A community's heart beats in the something special that makes it a desirable place to live, and that visitors describe to their friends when they return home.

What do people say about your community after visiting? What do they notice first when they come into town and what makes that first meal memorable? What is the heritage that you hope every child in your community cherishes? Has it become the combo plate at the fast food place, the cappuccino at the name brand coffee shop, or maybe the charm of a discount warehouse stocked full of this week's super sale items? Every community can choose for itself what it values and how to preserve those values over time. Those values form the basis for the heartbeat of your community – whether it's called sense of place, story, or theme, it's what makes it livable for residents and memorable for visitors.

Having HEART on a Large Scale

CURITIBA, BRAZIL

When you think about establishing or maintaining the heart or social integrity of a community, you might think a really big city is unlikely to get that done. Curitiba, Brazil, is a city of two million people in southern Brazil that refers to itself as, "the city of all of us." Others describe it as the "ecological city of Brazil." One recent survey asking people if they were happy with where they lived found 99% of the people in Curitiba feel they are in the right place. Few other cities in the world can make such a claim.

In 1965 a young architect and planner, Jaime Lerner, worked on a Master Plan for Curitiba. He would later serve as mayor of the city for three terms and Governor of the State of Paraná in which Curitiba is located. Mayor Lerner and the Urban Planning Institute of Curitiba (IPPUC) set this growing community on a different course than most growing urban areas with the usual challenges. He was unique in being both a skilled planner and visionary leader for the community. Lerner once said, "They were trying to throw away the story of the city." He understood and protected the relationship between the city "story" and lifestyles of local people even though the city was growing and changing rapidly.

The average income in Curitiba is only around $2,500 USD but quality of life

Carlos Eduardo

Curitiba, Brazil, has taken steps to take a holistic look at urban planning and design.

is high in the city and crime rates are low. It is a pedestrian-friendly community where cars do not dominate the cityscape. Buses serve people with low fares for trips up to 70 kilometers. The 28 parks provide places to enjoy nature. The Rua Quinze, an important historic area in downtown, became a walking mall after the original plans for an auto overpass were discarded.

The "Green Exchange," a creative recycling program, gives bus tickets and food in exchange for garbage. More than 70% of the waste stream is recycled in the community. Homeless people and recovering alcoholics can find work in this hybrid of an environmental and social program. Children can exchange recyclables for school supplies, toys, chocolates, and show tickets.

Curitiba is described as one of the best examples in the world of a "sustainable community." An integrated approach to urban planning that starts with articulation of strong, local core values in a city plan has been instrumental in creating a community that cares for itself. Equally important has been the creation of an independent municipal authority to provide continuity in implementation of plans and continue research to improve future efforts.

—Tim Merriman

What are the benefits of establishing sense of place?

For many communities, short-term economics has been a critical driver for decision-making by developers and government entities. Unfortunately, the decision to focus on short-term gains often erodes the stability of a community over the long term.

The Brundtland Commission of the United Nations published *Our Common Future* in 1987, defining sustainability as "development that meets the needs of the present without compromising the ability of future generations to meet their own needs." John Elkington of the EarthLife Foundation is regarded by many as the first person to promote the idea that companies need to concern themselves not only with shareholders, but a broader range of stakeholders, referred to as the Triple Bottom Line (TBL) of economic, social, and ecological indicators.

> The Brundtland Commission of the United Nations defines sustainability as "development that meets the needs of the present without compromising the ability of future generations to meet their own needs."

Some writers have used an alliterative approach, referring to economics, ecology and equity, or product, place, and people. Regardless of the terms used, the idea of the Triple Bottom Line is the consideration of the total impacts of all that we do without preference to one of the indicators over the others. Proponents, such as Hazel Henderson, author of *Paradigms of Progress*, believe that accounting should not just measure the Gross Domestic Product (GDP) to understand the success of a nation. Economic progress must be balanced with sustaining healthy communities and the natural environment. The nation of Bhutan actually measures Gross National Happiness (GNH).

UNESCO's Man and the Biosphere Programme (MAB) embraced TBL as a way of assessing impacts on biogeographic regions. As Dan Shilling points out in *Civic Tourism: The Poetry and Politics of Place*, success at the community level has traditionally been defined by economic interests such as the Chamber of Commerce or Convention and Tourism Bureau, and not by local residents. If economic success alone is considered, it often is achieved at the expense of environmental and social degradation. The Civic Tourism movement is based on finding balance in tourism development using TBL as a broader set of indicators, not just the churn of dollars or heads in beds. Shilling suggests that in tourism communities, TBL can and should be defined through civic engagement, allowing local people to define the core values of the community and identify what matters to them.

One of the leading examples in applying the Triple Bottom Line approach can be found in Seattle, Washington. In 1990, the Global Tomorrow Coalition organized a workshop in Seattle that led to the founding of Sustainable Seattle. This movement brought together a panel of over 150 civic leaders in 1992 to develop a set of indicators specific to Seattle. The panel included representatives from city and county government, business, environmental groups, students, educators, the religious community, and social activists. Together they agreed to and published twenty indicators of a healthy Triple Bottom Line in 1993. Over the next two years, the group identified 20 additional indicators and published their second report that was recognized a year later by the United Nations Centre for Human Settlements with an "Excellence in Indicators Best Performance."

CIVIC TOURISM
The Poetry and Politics of Place

Dan Shilling

Dan Shilling's book (2009) emphasizes the need for civic engagement in developing tourism opportunities.

The grassroots effort created a nonprofit corporation in 1997. By 1998, the city could identify trends using Sustainable Seattle's report card. Some of the key indicators such as air quality and volunteer involvement in schools are improving, while others are flat or trending downward. By providing a tool with which to track success, based on stated core values, community groups are empowered to identify issues of concern, collect data, and convey priorities to the city government.

Seattle's example demonstrates that a very large community can develop an

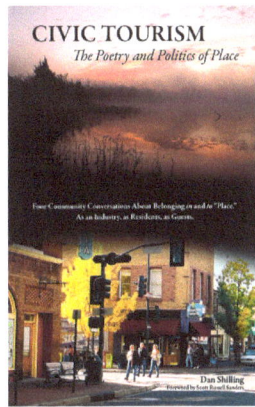

identity as a great place to live and wonderful place to visit, while working to maintain or improve what is desirable and move away from undesirable trends. It's a work in progress, but it has become an international model and resulted in many awards and greater investment by foundations to support this amazing collaborative effort at the community level. Margaret Mead, the great cultural anthropologist, said, "Never doubt that a small group of thoughtful, committed citizens can change the world. Indeed, it is the only thing that ever has."

By providing a tool with which to track success, based on stated core values, community groups are empowered to identify issues of concern, collect data, and convey priorities to the city government.

What threatens a sense of place?

In some communities, development seems to be a hunger that devours the quality of life. The very attractions courted as "progress" by local politicians become the reasons long-term residents move away when the economy changes and the heartbeat of the community begins to feel hypertensive, fueled by increasing traffic and the frustration of finding a parking space.

In 1990, Colorado voters approved casino gambling for a few select communities that needed an economic boost. Blackhawk, Central City and Cripple Creek changed quickly and dramatically from sleepy historic towns with little traffic into glitzy casino towns with big hotels and gaming. The authentic heritage attractions disappeared or changed under the pressure for more gaming areas and local people had to either adapt to the single economic driver of gambling or move. The economically-based strategy worked for the landowners who owned key properties but many people moved away to escape the frantic nightlife of casino towns. Although the tax base did in fact grow dramatically, these modern casino towns show little sign of measured growth or desirable social and environmental trends, ironically reliving their sustainable gold rush boom times.

Many communities that have decided (or been forced) to refocus their

The Ameristar Casino Resort Spa Black Hawk, located in Black Hawk, Colorado.

economic base on tourism alone have created an artificial sense of place but lost their sense of security and identity. The values most treasured by long-term residents can be marginalized while the values of short-term development, growth, and generification take over. Few people would be willing to trade an artificially inflated financial future for their community for the ability to live there and enjoy it. Carmel-by-the-Sea and Aspen in the U.S., Cannes and St. Tropez in France, Torremolinas and Benidorm in Spain, and many other tourist communities have lost not only their lower classes but also their middle class inhabitants. Some of these towns must now use buses to bring in a labor force to work at the cafés and lodging areas from bedroom communities that are more affordable. You can get too much of a good thing. Indeed you have to

Sustainable Seattle

WASHINGTON, USA

Since 1991, Sustainable Seattle has been a dynamic program in the Central Puget Sound area of the northwestern United States. They have worked actively with the 1987 definition of sustainability by the Brundtland Commission as "meeting the needs of the present without compromising the ability of future generations to meet their own needs." They state that *in practice, we seek to balance concerns for social equity, ecological integrity, and economic vitality – to create a livable community today while ensuring a healthy and fulfilling legacy for our children's children.*

Sustainable Seattle provides a model for the power of using civic engagement to create strategies embraced by social, environmental and economic stakeholders. Early in the process they identified indicators of sustainability and conducted the baseline research to determine the status of the community in each area. This grade card of "sustainability indicators" is now in its fourth iteration and is broken into four environments: natural, built, social and personal. With each one they track the trend as being away from sustainability, toward sustainability, staying the same or lacking in data to determine status.

Natural environment indicators focus on acres of high quality soils, acres of priority habitat, acres of protected land, air quality, wild salmon populations, safe/edible shellfish and a dozen other key indicators. In each case they focus on measurable results. Their website shows two decades of measurements on most parameters with specific discussion of the desirable change.

B-Sustainable, a project of Sustainable Seattle, gives practitioners and advocates the information they need to work together or separately to be effective in pursuit of desirable change. This collaborative effort includes:

Seattle's Pike Place Market

- A regional resource of relevant, trusted, and actionable information;

- A participatory process for identifying goals, indicators and actions based on cross-community dialogues;

- A framework that supports meaningful understanding of the sustainability challenges our region faces;

- A gateway to in-depth information including the latest research reports on regional sustainability issues; and

- A network for sharing information about our progress towards sustainability in the Central Puget Sound region

What keeps Sustainable Seattle sustainable? A very strong coalition of sponsors, partners and individuals support this effort that has lasted over two decades. Foundations, government agencies and industry collaborate in planning and implementation to work toward the changes they want.

—Tim Merriman

Sedona's stunning scenery is sometimes blocked by traffic jams and tourist traps at street level.

identify what "good things" you want to preserve or they may be the first to disappear when unregulated development occurs.

Development is not the only threat to a community's sense of place. The bigger threat is often that no one knows or agrees on the community's story. Often, city planners or individual developers make decisions without consideration of how such decisions might affect the way the resident or visiting public views the larger community. When civic leaders do not agree on or understand sense of place, it becomes impossible to address the Triple Bottom Line or create a sustainable community. What is the story that lies at the heart of your town? If the story's been lost along the road to development or worse yet, if no one knows what it is, it may be time to perform a heart transplant and bring your community back from the brink of generification.

How does a community develop a sense of place?

Sense of place can be defined by those who live and work in a community, or by visitors who bring expectations along with their luggage. Civic tourism is one of the movements in the United States that has risen out of the frustrations of communities that attempt to transform themselves into tourist destinations without retaining the genuine value and qualities that make them a desirable place to live. The concept of civic tourism originated in Arizona, with the work of Dan Shilling, author of *Civic Tourism: The Poetry and Politics of Place.* Civic tourism blends two points of view about sense of place by encouraging the development of healthy communities that will then also draw tourists, instead of creating tourism venues that ultimately cause problems for their communities.

In many communities, sense of place has become an artificial distinction promoted by chambers of commerce or convention and visitor bureaus that often see beds and heads as a simple solution to bringing revenue into the town. Pandering to the expectations of visitors at the expense of supporting the needs of residents creates communities that cannot sustain themselves over time. When the philosophy becomes "if you build it, they will come" the reality is often that "they" (the people who live there) will leave. Sedona, Arizona, is a good example of one of those romantic communities with a somewhat displaced sense of place. Once known primarily as a spiritual and artistic haven framed by a stunning red rock landscape, this community has undergone a decade of development that took it from small town chic to bustling tourist town. A home that would sell for $200,000 in many other Arizona communities could be as much as $800,000 in Sedona. Its quaint charm has given way to hectic success. A handful of artist galleries have become dozens and souvenir shops line the streets. The landscape hasn't changed, but it's harder to see behind the highly developed main street. The proliferation of tourism has brought prosperity for a few, and traffic jams for all.

Conventional wisdom in development seems to be to build more hotels, convention space, and restaurants and monetary success will surely follow as those facilities are filled. Build more golf courses and people will flock to the region to play. This approach may provide a short-term boost to a local economy, but rarely leads to long-term sustainability for a variety of reasons that developers looking for a quick economic surge may not consider. Once the community begins catering to tourists, the local residents may not be able to afford to live there. Golf courses can demand tremendous water resources, appeal to a narrow demographic and rarely develop around the unique social and environmental fabric of the area. More often

San Antonio Riverwalk

they convert native landscapes to bluegrass and seaside bentgrass at great expense and ignore the history of the landscape they have altered.

A 2005 study at Arizona State University found that heritage tourists stay four times as long as golf tourists. They are interested in an authentic experience when they visit a community. They invest in the heritage infrastructure of the community by visiting historic homes, museums, zoos, nature centers, parks and refuges. This is not to say that recreation venues like golf courses don't have a place in a community, but rather that they shouldn't necessarily drive the expenditure of funds within the community on the assumption that golfers will generate tourism dollars that will help the community. The same could be said for any proposed tourism development if it seems inappropriate for the size, environment, or story of a town.

While some communities evolve into interesting places, others plan the elements that become their "sense of place" trademarks, taking into consideration what makes them unique. San Antonio's Riverwalk is just a few blocks of businesses nestled around a very artificially channeled San Antonio River that actually gets drained and cleaned at certain times of the year. The amount of water that flows through it is modest. It is not a natural feature, impressive in size or grand in scale, but it has become legendary as the heart of the city, a place for conventions, weddings, parties and vacations due to the mix of lodging, restaurants, bars and events that capitalize on the unique Spanish, Mexican and Texan themes of the community. The Paseo del Rio has a feeling that is uniquely San Antonio with mariachi bands, stone bridges and walkways framing a river once plagued by flooding and now controlled by a tunnel under the city that carries away floodwaters.

Can any community create a sense of place? The answer is a qualified "yes," if the planning process focuses on authentic themes and features to define experiences that reinforce the community's uniqueness. Thoughtful planning can protect and project the core values of the community that matter most to both residents and visitors. The remainder of this book explores the HEART model for community experience planning, built around five components that must be considered in every setting, whether rural or urban, indigenous village, small town or big city. Using the HEART model will ensure that your community experiences are consistently Holistic, Engaging, Appropriate, Rewarding, and Thematic. The HEART concept not only encourages, but requires thoughtful communication and civic engagement during the planning process to ensure success. This book identifies the characteristics of each of the HEART components and provides suggested methodologies for implementation that, along with the case studies throughout the book, can serve as models for those attempting to put the heart back in their community.

> Thoughtful planning can protect and project the core values of the community that matter most to both residents and visitors.

19

Revitalization of Old Town Fort Collins

COLORADO, USA

Many communities see their original downtown decline as a place to shop or attend events as new developments occur in more convenient locations. The challenge of creating a strong sense of place in the traditional location of "downtown" can be difficult, especially if money is a barrier. Fort Collins, Colorado, struggled with this dynamic in "Old Town," the original downtown area as the community expanded. In the early 1980s, they found a way to do something about it.

Colorado law allows communities to form a downtown development authority (DDA), giving them unique abilities to finance projects they believe will enhance their downtown. Tax increment financing (TIF) uses the net new property tax revenues generated through property improvements resulting in an increase of assessed property value in the district. Fort Collins DDA was created in 1981 with the desire to restore Old Town as a place to live and visit. Business owners, property owners and residents of the district took part in the planning process.

Gene Mitchell, the developer of Old Town Square, believed they could create

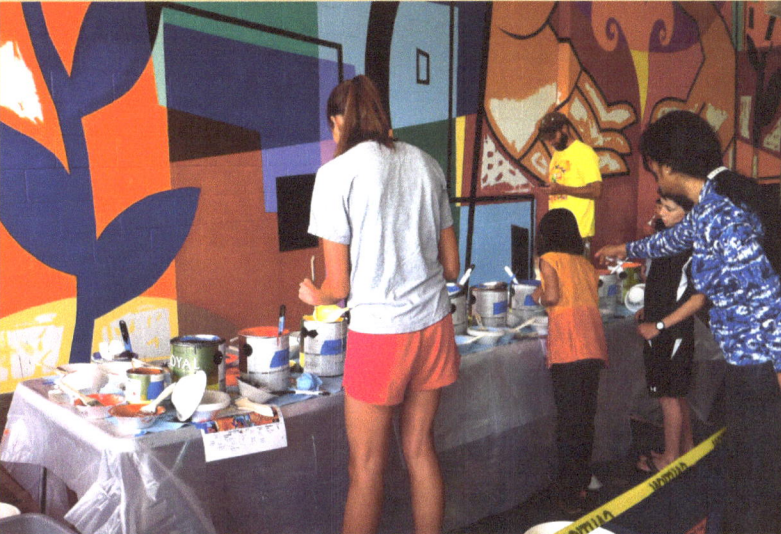

A community mural project in Fort Collins, Colorado, brings together people from diverse cultures to express their unity through art.

a space that would be an attraction for residents and tourists, based on his "strong feeling that this wonderful city needed a heart." He bought properties to consolidate the square area and obtained funding for street improvements and a parking garage from DDA. By 1985 the area was open, but the recession at the time made initial efforts challenging. The initial partnership broke up and the property ended up in foreclosure. A new management company was put into place and it slowly grew and became successful.

DDA's use of Tax Increment Funding gave businesses reason to locate in the downtown and develop services compatible with the area. DDA funds a variety of projects, including providing façade grants, and programs that help transform the image of the downtown. Beet Street (reflective of the history of the sugar beet industry in Fort Collins) is an arts program funded by DDA that brings more than 100 annual events to the Old Town Square area.

Fort Collins has become the kind of community that attracts and holds people who value an outdoor lifestyle. Old Town's outdoor cafes, brew pubs, boutiques and coffee shops are favored weekend and evening spots for college students, working professionals and ranch families in town for the day.

The dream of Gene Mitchell and his partners did eventually come true but not without considerable time, effort and collaboration.

—Tim Merriman

2   **Holistic**

The fabric of a community is a complex tapestry, with multiple interwoven threads. Thoughtful planning creates a community that can be compared to a work of art where every individual detail contributes to the overall pattern of that tapestry. Infrastructure, service quality, lodging options, food choices, and a variety of attractions work together to define the big picture. A community experience plan (CEP) suggests ways in which residents and tourists connect with a community and come to care about it. The CEP does not focus on any one museum, business, trail, or event, but holistically considers how people might use all services and facilities in loosely defined experience patterns.

How can thematic interpretation influence community planning?

For more than three decades heritage interpretation professionals have planned holistic experiences at parks, zoos, museums, nature centers, historic sites, botanical gardens, aquariums, and other interpretive sites (places where our natural and cultural heritage resources are explored by and interpreted to the public). Using the principles described in *Interpretive Planning: The 5-M Model for Successful Planning Projects* by Lisa Brochu (2003), agencies and organizations have moved from a strictly resource-based planning approach to more of a market-based planning approach built around communicating

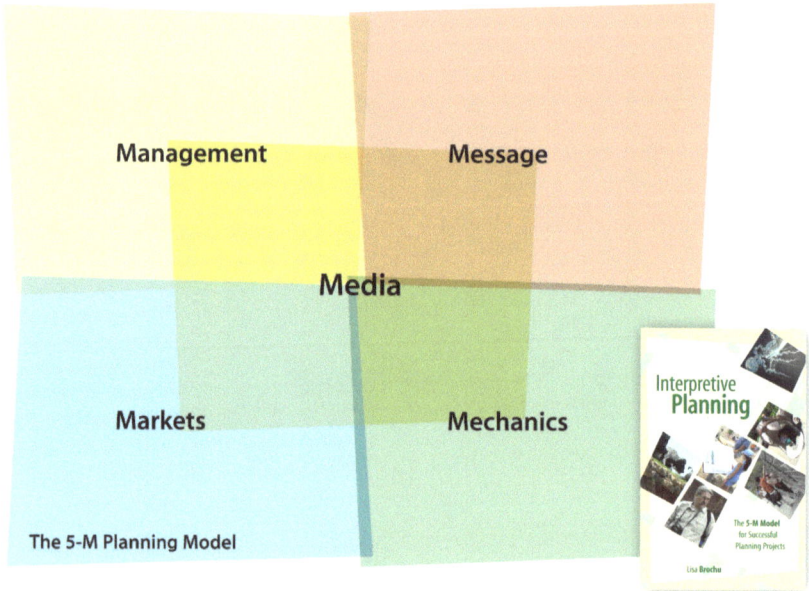

Figure 1. The five Ms outlined in Lisa Brochu's book
Interpretive Planning require consideration in the
planning process

a central theme or message to specific audiences to help accomplish management objectives. Expanding that process to an entire community allows diverse interests to come together around a central theme that conveys sense of place through retention of core values expressed by those who live and work in the community.

Creating great experiences built around a community's preferred lifestyles requires the consideration of several factors in the planning process that are similar to the interpretive planning process. Just like planning a new exhibit gallery at the museum or a special event at the nature center, it's not enough to have a great idea ... a good planner must also look at the management framework (policies, staffing, budget, facilities, etc.) that will provide the context and support that will sustain ongoing activities. It does no good to plan a visitor center with high-tech exhibits that requires multiple staff positions

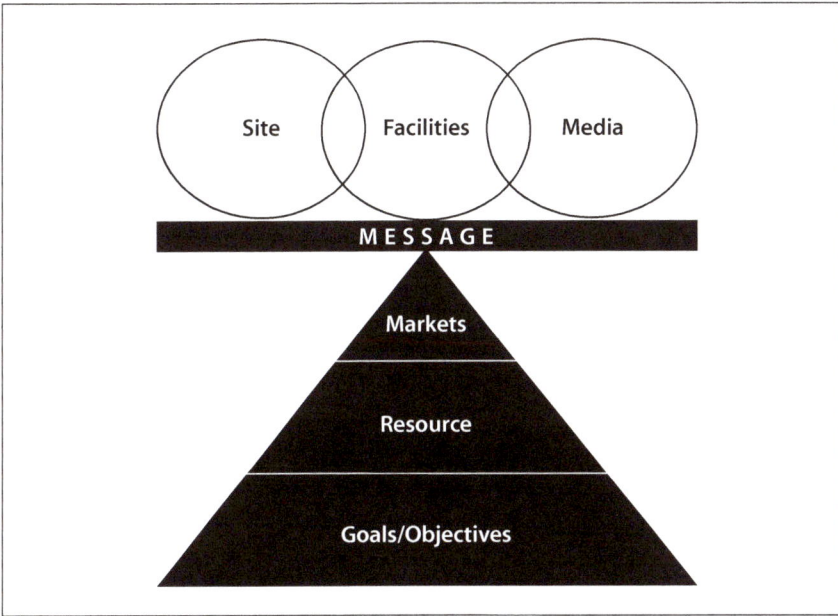

Figure 2. Design Balance Diagram

to operate if the community does not have the necessary staff or resources to hire or train the people needed to maintain such a facility. An interpretive plan must also include a thorough market analysis and thoughtful development of the message to be communicated about the resource (in this case, the resource might be the community's values) to varied audiences.

The same principles that frame an interpretive plan can be used on a community-wide or region-wide basis to create holistic experiences that contribute to the development or refinement of a sense of place attractive to residents and visitors alike.

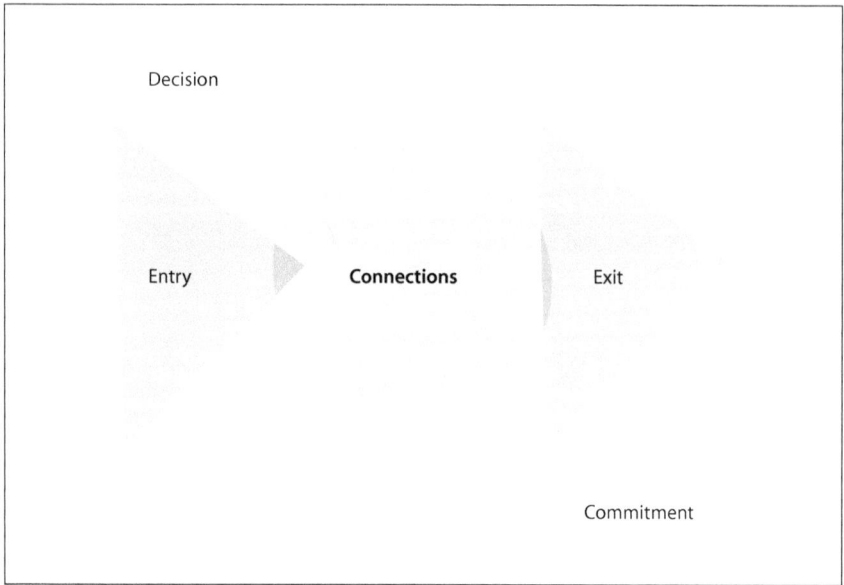

Figure 3. Visitor Experience Model

Understanding the basics of interpretive planning

An interpretive plan is built around two big concepts: Design Balance and Visitor Experience Design. Simply put, these two concepts establish the framework for providing interpretive opportunities that define the visitor experience at interpretive sites. Design Balance (Brochu, 2003) suggests that architecture (facilities), landscape architecture (site elements), and interpretive media (programming, exhibits, signs, etc.) should be planned and designed simultaneously for the most effective communication of a message based on the story behind the resource, the interests of the audience, and the objectives of management.

In preparing a Community Experience Plan, it is unlikely that these three elements of architecture, landscape architecture and media can be developed simultaneously, since most communities already have buildings and some infrastructure in place. However, new developments and redesigns can

A "Circle Farm Tour" sign in Canada identifies the historic site as part of a larger experience in the region. It provides directional information and serves as part of the entry experience in finding the site.

effectively take the principle of Design Balance (Figure 2) into consideration as the community reflects on its past and moves into the future.

Visitor Experience Design (Brochu, 2003) considers the sequencing of the various stages of the experience to create a meaningful event from beginning to end. The sequence begins with the decision a person makes to seek an experience and ends with an appropriate commitment to further thought or action. Between the decision and the commitment, the experience includes entry, connections, and exit phases.

The concept of Visitor Experience Design (Figure 3) applies equally well to visitors and residents when considering the application to a Community Experience Plan. The concept is scalable – a planner can look at a single program or event and think about how someone might experience just that event through the various phases. Or the planner can expand the concept to a site, such as a park, museum, zoo, or nature center. Or the planner can expand

Expanding an Interpretive Plan to Site, Community, or Regional Scope

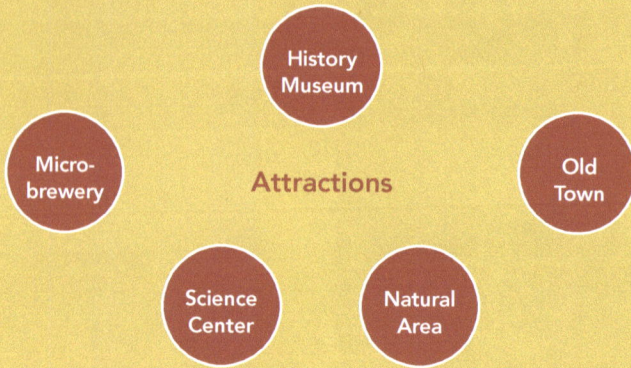

Each attraction in a community may have its own interpretive plan.

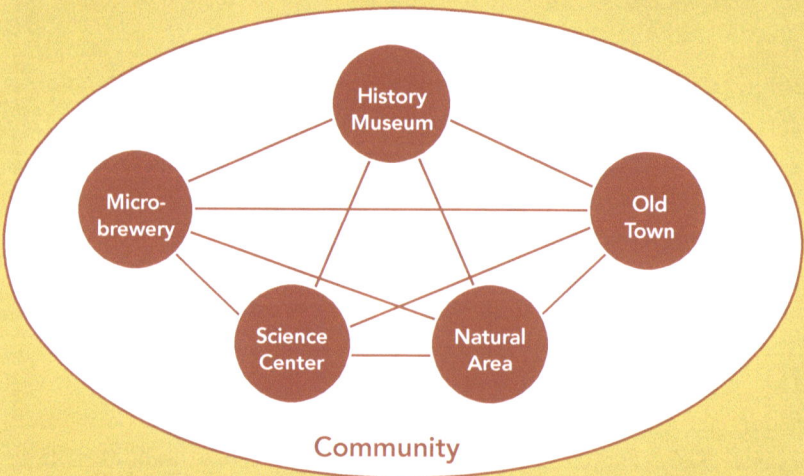

An overall community can create a comprehensive community experience plan with consideration of individual plans. This approach can also be expanded to include multiple communities in a corridor or loop such as a scenic byway.

Trail or Byway

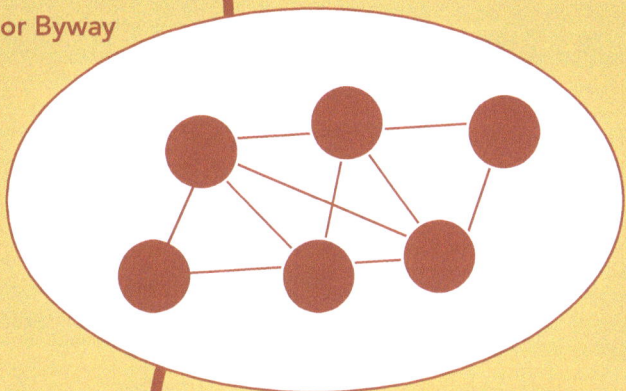

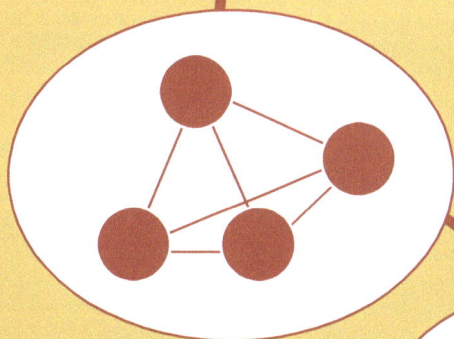

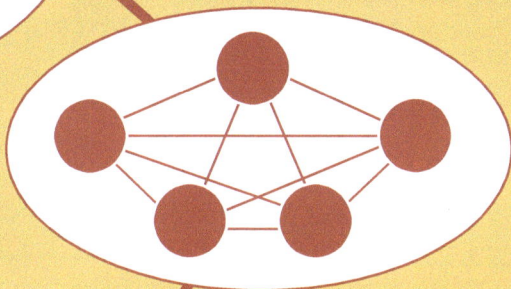

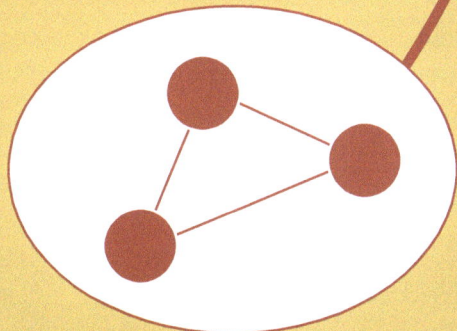

further to an entire community or include several communities into a Regional Experience Plan. To illustrate the concept, think about how someone from out of town might experience your community.

Tourists plan to visit a community based on the usual decision points. A friend recommended it, the convention brought them to it, the Internet search engine found it, the TV show promoted it, the tour company packaged it for them, or they saw an attractive billboard or heard an appealing advertisement while traveling that encourages them to detour from their original route to take advantage of a nearby opportunity. With that initial contact, expectations have been established, whether intentional or not.

The same is true of community experiences. Something has to get residents off their couches and into community events and locales. Whatever facilitates that decision—whether it's a neighbor's recommendation or a radio or television ad—creates expectations. The rule of thumb should always be to underpromise and overdeliver. Let people come to an experience and find that it is even better than they had hoped. That way, they become advocates and perhaps serve as someone else's decision point as they provide glowing reviews on the internet or among their friends.

Entry experiences can be many things, including the journey to the site. The drive time and what happens along the way set the stage for what is to come. Wall Drug Store in South Dakota combines decision point with their entry experience, by staging a series of highway billboards and Burma Shave style signs for over a hundred miles in every direction. By the time a visitor reaches Wall Drug, it's a must-do, because the experience has already begun. The entry experience can also include buffer zones, traffic into an area, signage, parking, landscaping, and the human host at the entry station or ticket booth. What's the first thing that people see, smell, hear, or feel when they sense that they have arrived? A well-designed and welcoming entry experience can plant the seeds of success in everything that follows. Conversely, a poorly planned entry can create disillusionment that starts a downhill slide of negativity that lasts throughout the remainder of the experience. A famous heritage community in the eastern U.S. has a sign at its parking area that suggests, "You cannot possibly see all of this area in less than two days." One can only assume that the intent of the sign is to give visitors a realistic expectation of the amount of time that can be invested in a thorough visit. But for many visitors, the sign means that an hour or an afternoon is not going to provide a good experience, so why bother if that's all the time there is? The entry fee is high and it's just as easy to go somewhere else. The sign acts as a deterrent, turning away many who might find this a fascinating place but who won't take a chance when there are more predictable half-day experiences nearby.

The *connections phase* provides the opportunity for the visitor to make emotional and intellectual connections with the resource or community. This phase offers the visitor an appropriate mix of media that will encourage interaction with the community through participation in programs, at local businesses, with exhibits, on trails, or any number of other ways that communicate your sense of place or the message you're sending about your community. In some cases, it may simply mean providing access to self-directed experiences (as in the case of a wilderness area that can only be experienced directly by back-country hikers or paddlers), but in others, it may require providing consistent message elements through facility design, landscaping, and the variety of experiences available in your community. Think about the disconnect that occurs for visitors if one of your community's core values is environmental responsibility and yet all city landscaping requires high maintenance that may be environmentally destructive because non-native species have been planted.

> The CEP serves the community in several ways, as an assessment tool, a planning tool, a funding tool, and an evaluation tool.

The *exit phase* is that last impression that occurs as a visitor leaves. It may be just as important as the first impression, because it can provide the opportunity to engage people in thinking about the message behind the experience while on the journey or upon arrival at their home. The exit phase very often includes the opportunity to purchase mementoes. While your community may not be able to control all items that are sold as souvenirs, there are beachside communities who have successfully banned the use of plastic bags in souvenir shops and grocery stores because of the danger to marine animals as an example of their commitment to environmental stewardship. These sorts of actions can make a significant difference in how visitors perceive your community. Are visitors anxious to leave or do they feel welcome to linger or return? The exit phase sets up that final phase that helps measure your success – commitment.

The *commitment* that a visitor makes is a personal decision, but the planner can set objectives that help define the type of commitment that would be desirable. For example, perhaps your community would like assistance (financial or otherwise) with a specific program for disadvantaged youth or restoration of an historic building. The connection that has been made with your visitors (or residents) can spur their commitment to helping with your community project. Maybe the commitment made is more along the lines of returning for another visit or placing a positive review on a travel website. Although you cannot always predict the outcome of any one visit, your planning should include thinking about what the desired outcome would be and then crafting community experiences that might enable visitors and residents to make an appropriate personal commitment.

What's the point of a Community Experience Plan?

A Community Experience Plan combines the concepts of the VEM and the DBM to enable the planner to look at the community as a whole with several significant components. If you consider that each interpretive facility or neighborhood or business zone is one of those components, the CEP provides the framework for linking each to the other in "experience packages" that help visitors or residents make sense of the community. In other words, the CEP is an organizer that identifies commonalities between individual parts to provide a holistic view of the community that is greater than the sum of its separate parts.

The CEP serves the community in several ways:

- An *assessment tool* to identify current strengths and weaknesses

- A *planning tool* to identify ways in which desired outcomes might be achieved within a given time frame

- A *funding tool* with which to garner support for strategic initiatives

- An *evaluation tool* to measure success

What makes the CEP different from other community planning efforts is the emphasis on unifying diverse interests around a central theme or message. While some urban and regional planners focus on economics or ergonomics to ensure the biggest return on investment or efficiency of action, the CEP focuses on holistic thematic experiences, which are truly the heart of any great community. Like all the pieces of the HEART model, the extent of holism that currently exists or could exist in your community is a subjective matter. But you've probably visited places that made you feel good about the visit even if you couldn't put your finger on why. Usually it's because thoughtful planning has created linkages – visually, physically, thematically – that help express the sense of place and support the core values of the community.

The Eiffel Tower creates instant recognition for the city of Paris.

Street markets that open in the darkness of early morning and close by early afternoon are part of the authentic Paris.

The Arche de Triomphe, Notre Dame Cathedral and the Louvre Museum - iconic symbols of Paris.

La Patisserie, or the French pastry shop, produces baked goods that delight the eyes as well as the palette.

Tourist buses charge one fee for several days of "hop on and hop off" use and include optional earphone audio tours in a variety of languages.

Sidewalk cafes provide a place for residents and tourists to relax, watch the flow of life and enjoy incredible food.

Boutique hotels, more common than franchise hotels, are even more charming because they are usually more affordable and unique.

Boat traffic on the Seine River includes tour boats, restaurants, working boats and floating homes.

Mto wa Mbu

TANZANIA

Mto wa Mbu (Mosquito Creek) is a unique community in central Tanzania that proudly provides tours through its Cultural Tourism Programme. Tourists on their way to Lake Manyara National Park, Ngorogoro Conservation Area and Serengeti National Park pass through this community, but if they stop, they will find a unique experience with a variety of options.

Tanzania has more than 120 tribes and all are represented in the community. An irrigation project in the 1950s created opportunities in this rural village and the government encouraged people to move to this kind of area where social services could be provided more efficiently. In 1995 SNV – The Netherlands Dutch Development Organisation assisted the Tanzania Tourism Board in developing programs to provide benefits to local people. The community was involved in planning the tours to be offered and they manage the resulting programs.

We took part in one of these well-designed tours. Orientation and introductions began at a local café followed by a slow meander through the community marketplace. Mingling with the vendors of local foods and goods

A local guide takes tourists into the village's marketplace and explains the importance of the variety of bananas sold to residents.

and their shoppers allowed us to see the community from the inside instead of through a tourist venue.

The next stop was the home brewery of a local Chaga family. There we learned the unique story of how this special brew based on bananas is key in marriage negotiations, friendships, and conflict resolution. We passed a mug of banana beer to share amongst our fellow travelers and then followed a trail through a banana grove to learn about the thirty varieties of banana grown for varied food uses. We also visited a community of local artists and another of woodcarvers and many in our group bought craft items and artwork from them. The hike ended with a lunch prepared by local women that enabled us to share in the diverse food cultures in the community.

The guides emphasized that Mto wa Mbu is a place where people from diverse backgrounds work and live together in harmony. They explained that people in Tanzania are tribal in origin but think of themselves as Tanzanians first and then as members of their tribes. That theme for the experience held up very well and we left with a greater understanding of Tanzania and the local community.

Photo Essay

Bar Harbor consciously maintains a historic look and feel throughout the community to create a unique identity for the area.

Tours on the water offer a variety of important attractions for coastal towns with whale watching being one of the most popular.

A tour of lobster traps and seal rocks in Bar Harbor may be an interesting and more reliable option when whales are not easily seen.

Kayak tours appeal to more active tourists who want an intimate experience with the water and wildlife.

Local cafes provide unique, affordable food experiences for local residents and visitors, capitalizing on the readily available lobster harvest.

Supporting a local nonprofit organization that protects moose populations has a promotional value for this store.

Kansas Wetlands & Wildlife National Scenic Byway

KANSAS, USA

The Kansas Wetlands & Wildlife National Scenic Byway is 77 miles long in rural central Kansas. It includes three counties, seven communities and three separate wetlands/wildlife areas. The communities range in population from 154 to 15,000. Ownership of the wetlands is just as varied with one being state owned, one federally owned, and one owned by a not-for-profit organization.

The byway steering committee oversees the byway and its corridor management plan (required for designation as a National Scenic Byway). Because of the diverse interests of the stakeholders involved, the committee developed an emphasis on partnership. Therefore, every county, community (regardless of size), and wildlife area has a representative on the steering committee. Each has only one representative so they speak as equals. We have found this to be a thing of beauty and power. Since they come to the table as equals within the steering committee structure, the individuals on the committee move in an agreed-upon direction and speak with one consistent voice and message.

Cheyenne Bottoms

The crafting of the byway "foundation statement" for the Corridor Management Plan reflected the strength of the partnerships from the very beginning. It reads:

> The Kansas Wetlands and Wildlife Scenic Byway includes conservation and promotion of the resources along the designated route and provides management of the route by local jurisdictions for economic development and long term resource protection.

The development of this scenic byway came from a county economic development strategic planning summit. Tourism is recognized as an important factor in economic development since "quality of life" and "tourism" elements are almost a complete duplicate for communities. In other words, what creates quality of life is what also draws tourists. So, economic development for the rural communities was a high priority for the counties.

The byway received designation for the intrinsic quality of "nature" based largely on the three wetlands areas located on the byway which have all been designated as "wetlands of international importance." Therefore, conservation and protection of the wetlands were important factors as well.

We have always been clear that the development of tourism and visitor experiences will NEVER be at the expense of the resource. Again, this clarification and "speaking as one voice" by the byway has strengthened the partnerships involved.

The foundation statement has also provided clear direction for product development as it relates to the byway. We understand that many byways receive designation – put up their signs – and begin promotion. This has not been our philosophy. We chose to move somewhat more slowly but with thoughtful consideration.

Interpretation for the byway was deemed to be our first priority. While the steering committee always spoke as "one voice" we understood the importance of having our message widespread throughout the entire byway corridor. However, if we wanted all partners to consistently speak with one voice – telling the same story – we needed to make sure the byway story was developed and known. Public meetings were held in all communities to gather ideas for story lines. Input was also sought from refuges staff. A theme statement was developed for the byway along with five sub-themes. The theme statement, "Everywhere you look, you see evidence of motion and change," and the five subthemes, tied directly to the intrinsic quality for which the byway received designation. The subthemes related the many ways in which motion and change are exhibited: migrating birds, human habitation over centuries, geologic features that change the landscape, etc. A variety of storylines were listed for each of these subthemes. Interpretation for the byway revolved around

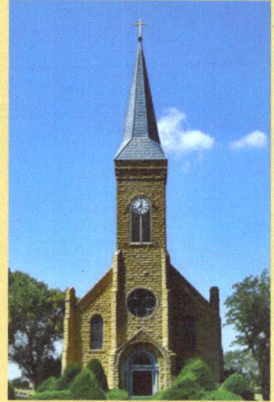

Beccy Tanner

The byway corridor community of Claflin (pop. 705) has adopted the topic of geology. This will serve as the introduction to tour state historic bridges and tell the story of post rock.

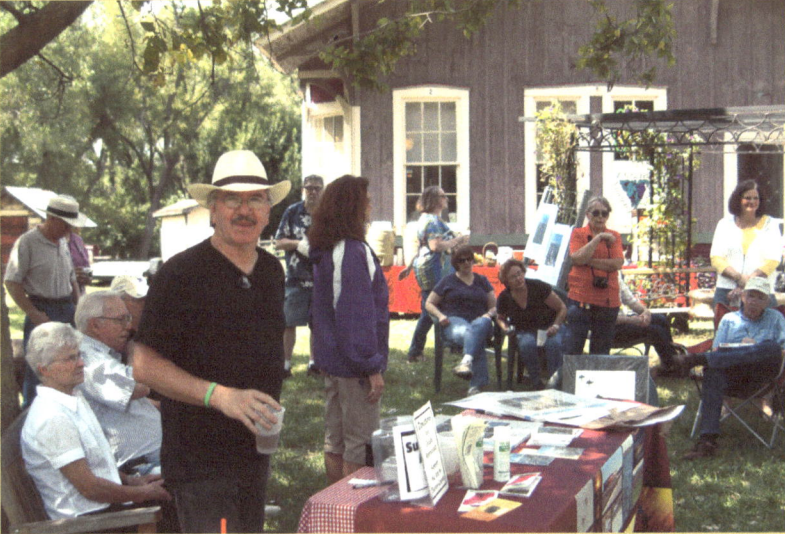

Artist reception at Dozier Winery outside the byway corridor community of Ellinwood (pop. 2,048).

this theme and sub-themes through an interpretive plan, signage, website, and byway guide.

Next came marketing. Extensive national market research was done to determine appropriate niche markets for this byway. We felt a really targeted approach to the appropriate niche markets would be far more productive than a "shotgun" approach. On completion of market research, the committee developed a sustainable long-term marketing plan. Again, we went to our theme statement and the interpretive universal concepts to determine a marketing platform.

Meetings have been held in all seven corridor communities to deliver the findings of the market research and the marketing plan developed with that material.

A different sub-theme will be adopted and developed by each of the communities. This will allow them to tell their community story as it relates to the byway and the overall theme statement. Additional communities do not feel like they are in competition since each focuses on a unique aspect that relates them to the byway. This approach has opened the door for the development of an internal marketing team that will focus on "cross-marketing" between the communities.

A national marketing management team has also been assembled that will focus strictly on delivering the message to the seven niche markets on a national level.

All of this has taken us about four years to set in place. However, it is the approach we feel to be right for all those concerned. The worst thing possible for a visitor is for an attraction/area/byway/community . . . to oversell and under deliver. And, we had said at the very beginning . . . "never at the expense of the resource". The best way to ensure this is thoughtful planning.

The most significant victory to date I can report is that EVERYONE is excited. The wildlife areas have benefited from the partnerships developed with the communities and community-based initiatives are becoming part of the "one voice – one story" team.

—Cris Collier, Great Bend Convention and Visitors Bureau

3

Engaging

Holistic experiences appeal to the whole person. Is there a place or event in your life experience that calls you back again and again – somewhere or sometime that your brain takes you to when it drifts into a dream state? Most people have had some sort of rich experience in their lifetimes, the kind that makes you want to repeat it, whether to explore the memory of it more deeply or just to feel the intensity of it all over again.

The human brain is interesting in that it is really two brains: in simple terms, the left cerebral hemisphere or left brain stores information and the right brain stores experiences. Without conscious effort, the whole brain continually integrates information about the world by putting it into context with our emotional understanding of the situation. When something excites or frightens us, neurologists suggest that our brain chemicals are so stimulated that they capture the moment so that we become capable of remembering every detail of the situation. The smells, the tastes, the feelings and other contextual or emotional elements are imprinted, ready to draw on in the future as needed. This is how we learn from experiences, so that in the future we can avoid disastrous actions or encourage healthy ones.

Advertisers have always understood the power of engaging interest by making emotional connections. Companies could advertise only the tangible qualities of their products and appeal to the intellect of their customers, but if you watch television or analyze written advertising, you're likely to notice the use of those intangible ideas that tug at consumer heartstrings. Car companies, for example, rarely talk about the materials used in construction of their vehicles. Instead, they talk about how the car's features relate to you: the power of the car (you'll become more powerful if you own that car), the environmental aspects (you'll be a good environmental citizen if you own the car), or the safety devices (you'll be a better parent if you keep your children safe with this car).

Tangible qualities represent those things that are factual, the things that you can touch, taste, see, smell, or measure. Intangible ideas represent those bigger concepts that tangible qualities might evoke based on the personal filters of our experiences.

Because our brains tend to integrate left brain logic (tangible things) with right brain remembrance (intangible ideas), engagement usually occurs without any conscious effort on our part. However, as successful advertisements demonstrate, you can also influence the level of intellectual and emotional engagement by the choices you make in how you frame information.

Intangible ideas can sometimes be considered "universal concepts" if they are so common that any culture could embrace and understand them. Family, birth, death, life – although they may be treated differently in different cultures, every culture has some understanding of these and other concepts. Universal concepts are often considered the most powerful in making engaging people emotionally because everyone can relate to them in some way. Movie trailers make good use of universal concepts as they attempt to pique the interest of the public in widespread appeals. They talk about adventure, love, power, home and other common denominators that speak to the human condition.

How do we engage people in the community with emotional and intellectual experiences?

People often describe experiences as "been there, done that," meaning they don't need to repeat the event. Once was enough, or in some cases, more than enough. Think about the last time you visited another town and asked about things to do. If you talk to someone who grew up in the town, their perspective on what might be interesting may be quite different than yours. There is a tendency to get complacent about your own backyard. But imagine the difference if the experiences to be had in a community are interesting to tourists and residents alike.

The emotional impact of great experiences is hard to measure, but it does play out in measurable ways. If people enjoy a community and feel connected to it in a special way they may tell their friends about their experience, become volunteers, buy memorabilia, or donate to locate charitable organizations. Residents might remain in the community for generations, while visitors might extend their stay or return more often. Communities that encourage repeat visitation rarely have to expand their advertising budget. When people crave the available experiences over and over again, they sell themselves and others through word of mouth and Internet testimonials. Those are all measurable outcomes of people feeling connected. If you've ever left a museum, zoo or nature center and thought, "I don't need anything, but I'm going to buy something in the gift shop in appreciation and support for what they do here," then you've just made an emotional commitment to that facility.

> Information by itself, the intellectual connection, is not enough to fully engage people.

You didn't decide to buy something because of the information you picked up, but because you *felt* that the information mattered to you.

According to behavioral psychologist Dr. Sam Ham, there is no social science research that supports the notion that learning alone leads to loving. In fact, there is some evidence that suggests that if you are forced to learn something, you may become an expert, but you may actually come to dislike that subject. You may know someone who is excellent in a chosen field, but wishes desperately he or she could be doing something else that he or she truly loves. Information by itself, the intellectual connection, is not enough to fully engage people. You can even determine whether the information has been assimilated through cognitive testing, but if there is no emotional context for that information, it may simply get stored somewhere in the library of the left brain and never used. Providing statistics about your community (how many hotels, restaurants, and museums, etc.) without the emotional engagement of sharing a message about your core values does nothing to help residents or visitors feel connected to those values. If you have little concern over the future of your community, then engendering a connection may not be important. But if you hope to engage residents and visitors in helping your community sustain or improve the quality of life it offers, then

Local residents view Barton Springs as an important icon that represents the environmental attitude promoted in Austin, Texas.

making connections matters a great deal. This concept is what lies behind the theory of social marketing.

According to the United Kingdom's National Social Marketing Centre, social marketing can be described as the systematic application of marketing, along with other concepts and techniques, to achieve specific behavioral goals for a social good. Essentially, the social marketing construct suggests that if you can move people from being mildly curious about your community to caring about it, they will begin to care *for* it and its core values. For this construct to be successful, there is an important step between curiosity and caring - they must come to an understanding of why the community and its values matter to them. This step requires that you make an investment in creating the emotional connection that takes someone from simple knowledge to the deeper understanding that comes through experiential engagement.

Creating connections with tangible things and intangible ideas

A study of pool users at Barton Springs in Austin, Texas, reveals that few are first-time users. This natural cold-water spring has been a gathering place since its early discovery by Native Americans. As Austin has grown, Barton Springs remains an icon of the environmentally-based core values of the community. The study results are interesting because they point out that this unique feature is a place that draws community members as repeat visitors. It's a local favorite. So where do the few first-time users come from? Most are guests of the repeat visitors who have been let in on the "secret" of this not-so-hidden treasure, but some are visitors that have heard of Barton Springs from travel websites or from friends who have visited Austin. You could describe Barton Springs by listing its year-round average water temperature (68 degrees), its unique wildlife (the endangered Barton Springs salamander), its size (3 acres within a city center park), or its namesake (William Barton). But what people remember most about Barton Springs is far more intangible: the shock of swimming in icy cold water on a steaming hot day; the relaxing, laid-back atmosphere of those sunning on the grassy slope next to the pool; the sense of family and community that hangs in the sultry summer air. If you look at user reviews of Barton Springs Pool on the Internet, the most common phrase that turns up is "This IS Austin" or something that reflects that sentiment. That intangible, emotional connection to a valued resource is priceless in preserving Austin's sense of place, as residents take great pains to protect water quality throughout the area.

The Kohala Center

HAWAI'I, USA

We were first introduced to The Kohala Center at Kahalu'u Beach Park, one of our favorite snorkeling beaches on the Big Island of Hawai'i. Volunteers in blue ReefTeach T-shirts greet people as they enter the water and question visitors to determine their knowledge of reef life and etiquette. They use plastic field guide cards to acquaint people with the local ecosystem and help them understand the importance of not standing on the coral or handling the fragile creatures of the shallow bay. Benefits to life in the bay are evident to those who have watched degraded areas improve in recent years.

ReefTeach is only a small component of the education and research programs of The Kohala Center. Citizen Scientists have been taught to take water samples at Kahalu'u Bay to monitor the overall health of this rich ecosystem.

The center also has 45 community gardens at schools all over the island to encourage more families to eat locally grown food and learn more about traditional Hawaiian foods. The Hawai'i Island School Garden Network (HISGN) website gives island residents a place to learn of programs, monitor projects and get involved.

Kohala Center uses community volunteers as part of ReefTeach to host exhibits at Kahalu'u Beach Park that engage cruise boat passengers and other visitors in learning about reef ecology.

Some of the educational projects support doctoral and post-doctoral work by Native Hawaiians who direct their research efforts toward a better understanding of the cultural and natural landscapes, history, politics and society of the island, funded by the Andrew W. Mellon Foundation and King Kamehameha Schools.

Another program of The Kohala Center, in cooperation with The Brown University Environmental Leadership Lab (BELL), brings island high school students into a week-long program with twenty teenagers from all over the U.S. to learn on the land. They camp, attend Native Hawaiian cultural programs, do public service work, learn about native plants, go kayaking to learn about coral reefs and take part in varied leadership activities.

These and other ambitious programs of The Kohala Center grew out of community education efforts at the end of the twentieth century. Communities in northern Hawaii held forums in 1999–2000 that resulted in public health officials sharing alarming news. High rates of drug and alcohol abuse, domestic violence, and diabetes were increasingly evident in this tropical paradise, forcing community leaders to ask what would make for a happier and healthier community.

They identified three important goals:

1. greater educational opportunities for island youth;

2. assurance that adults—especially young adults—are qualified for the new jobs that ought to be coming to the island; and

3. a diversified economy.

They stated their mission as: *to respectfully engage the Island of Hawai'i as an extraordinary and vibrant research and learning laboratory for humanity.*

Their vision is: *a state of pono, in which individuals realize their potential, contributing their very best to one another, to the community, and to the 'āina [the land] itself, in exchange for a meaningful and happy life.*

This extraordinary vision for living in harmony with the land while seeking responsible, sustainable development for their communities has led to incredible success. The Kohala Center was formally introduced in January 2001 at a breakfast with a presentation by researchers, Professor Peter Vitousek, Professor Oliver Chadwick and Professor Louis Derry on "Hawaii as the Model Ecosystem of the World." This blend of education and research has grown from year one budget of $7,600 to more than 4.1

A ReefTeach volunteer chats with visitors as they enter the water to explain how they might protect the resource while snorkeling and swimming.

million dollars in FY2009/2010. The KHC staff of 36 under the leadership of Dr. Matt Hamabata as Executive Director now works with 20 partners and hundreds of volunteers to pursue their vision and the results are evident.

—Tim Merriman

Kahalu'u Beach Park is a coral reef with diverse fish populations but the shallow water permits coral to be trampled by uninformed snorkelers. Kohala Center has installed signs that help visitors understand the fragile ecosystem.

Kohala Center encourages local schools to grow taro in traditional wetland gardens to help children learn about their native Hawaiian heritage.

GreenTown: Creating Opportunities from Adversity

GREENSBURG, KANSAS

On May 4, 2007, the rural community of Greensburg, Kansas, was devastated by a tornado. More than 90% of the infrastructure, homes and businesses were destroyed. The community could have simply rebuilt with insurance and government assistance. That would have been enough for many but they did more. They worked together toward a shared dream.

Daniel Wallach and Catherine Hart, husband and wife, took a concept paper to the first community meeting held in Greensburg after the tornado, one week after the fact. Daniel had come up with the idea to offer the couple's services to the town's leaders if they would be interested in building back as a model green community. At the meeting they heard then-mayor Lonnie McCollum announce to the assembled group of 500 citizens that Greensburg was coming back bigger, better, and sustainably. Right after the meeting, Daniel and Catherine began meeting with city leaders and sharing the concept paper, and in short order the nonprofit Greensburg GreenTown was launched by the couple. GreenTown starting working right away to help local residents and business owners understand what it would take to "go green" and in the process helped de-politicize and demystify the concept.

One of the community's most important partners in the rebuilding sustainably has been with the U.S. Department of Energy's (DOE) National Renewable Energy Lab (NREL) in Golden, Colorado. Lynn Billman led a team of technologists and analysts in assisting civic leaders, local business owners, and families in rebuilding "green." Greensburg GreenTown's website at www.greensburggreentown.org includes a database of sustainable buildings which is maintained in conjunction with NREL. They describe NREL's involvement as "government at its best."

GreenTown's Silo House.

GreenTown serves as the green visitors center for the community. Staff provides tours of the community, educational programs, special events, and blog articles. Silo Eco-Home is the first of a series of eco-lodges being built in the community for visitors, with Meadowlark House slated for completion in early 2012. GreenTown's GreenTour Book tells the story of their journey in print and can be downloaded on the organization's website.

Natural disasters are going to happen each year but the locations of floods, tsunamis, tornadoes, and hurricanes are unpredictable. GreenTown creators hope to export this idea of going from adversity to sustainability. Their example is an excellent place to look if your community is rebuilding for any reason.

Bath, England, in the United Kingdom is famous for the ancient Roman baths.

Georgian architectural sites such as The Crescent and Circus by architect James Wood and his son can be found throughout the city.

Over 70 licensed volunteer tour guides (long-term local residents) share the rich history of the city.

FREE WALKING TOURS START HERE

The city posts times for walking tours of the historic district.

Impromptu entertainers add interest to the narrow medieval streets, but do not necessarily reflect the themes or history of the community.

Pizza Hut, like of the several franchise businesses in Bath, operates from either historic buildings or new structures built in traditional style from the local limestone used for centuries in the community.

Monterey, California brings people close to the water and wildlife of this scenic area.

Murals keep the literary works of John Steinbeck in the forefront of this community that figures prominently in his works.

The Monterey Bay Aquarium, in Cannery Row, attracts millions of people annually from all over the world.

Even the messages on sewer grates remind people that protection of water resources is everyone's responsibility.

The Monterey Bay Aquarium's Seafood Watch program encourages restaurants in Monterey and worldwide to participate in a thoughtful conservation program for sustainable fisheries.

Various local organizations cooperate in protection of sea otters in the bay.

4 Appropriate

Holistic experiences that engage people emotionally and intellectually must be **appropriate**, for the audiences that may be involved and in terms of authenticity. Community Experience Planning requires a thoughtful knowledge of the audiences that live in or visit the community or that may be desirable residents or visitors. Existing and potential audiences have specific preferences and beliefs. The more you know about them, the better you can design for them, always remaining conscious of protecting the way of life that the local community values.

Audiences can be defined in many ways. Essentially, an audience is any group of individuals for whom an experience, message, or media piece is designed. Market research is one obvious way to learn more about existing and potential audiences, but there are a number of ways in which to conduct market research. Some communities elect to hire a firm that specializes in market research. Such a contract can be time-consuming and expensive, but generally yields thorough and reliable results. Perhaps your community cannot afford a market research

> An audience is any group of individuals for whom an experience, message, or media piece is designed.

firm and an extensive study, but it also cannot afford to move forward with planning without some information about the audiences to be addressed.

Existing demographic data from the census can be helpful, as can other information that may be available from the state tourism office or from the Statewide Comprehensive Outdoor Recreation Plan (SCORP) that is conducted on a statewide basis every five years as one of the administrative requirements of the Land and Water Conservation Fund (LWCF) administered by the National Park Service. SCORP plans offer strategic focus for the expenditure of LWCF funds at the local level and contain useful data on trends in recreation and tourism in a given state. Using these established sources of data provide a big-picture backdrop for planning efforts, but civic engagement in the planning process is critical to success as it provides more immediate information about what might be appropriate for a given community.

A thoughtful civic engagement approach will bring together diverse interests from the community to develop consensus around core values, messages and what kinds of experiences are reasonable and sustainable.

Civic engagement may mean different things to different people, but the definition provided by the American Psychological Association of "individual and collective actions designed to identify and address issues of public concern" serves the concept of Community Experience Planning well. A thoughtful civic engagement approach will bring together diverse interests from the community to develop consensus around core values, messages and what kinds of experiences are reasonable and sustainable. Too often single interests choose either golf, car racing, IMAX theatres, conventions, or something similar to build a stronger economy because those things have been economic drivers in other communities, without overall acceptance of these ventures by the multiple interests involved in a community. These ventures may or may not bring the desired economic prosperity and may actually create other problems for the community that surface after the fact because concerns were not previously addressed through a reasonable civic engagement process.

What is appropriate for the community? What do life-long residents want for the future of their families? What core values of the community do we wish to protect? Dan Shilling points out that the tourism bureau in most communities is centered in the Chamber of Commerce, resulting in an emphasis on the short-term economic gains of tourism development without consideration of long-term social and environmental impacts. The natural allies of the tourism bureau should be natural and cultural heritage sites, organizations and community development interests that involve community residents. Shilling suggests that we reframe tourism development with a triple bottom line approach, appropriate for the community and the tourists served. This usually requires someone to take the lead and make an effort to bring key stakeholders together to consider options and plan together.

> The natural allies of the tourism bureau should be natural and cultural heritage sites, organizations and community development interests that involve community residents.

Appropriateness also suggests a need for authenticity. Community development should include a process of identifying the real natural and cultural stories of the area – what makes this place what it is? Every community has authentic places and experiences, but some choose to fabricate stories and experiences that seem more appealing. Often they are emulating a successful community whose development they admire. Being unique and true to the natural and cultural history of your community is a more enduring choice. These stories are what provide the basis for your community's primary message or theme, so being thoughtful and honest about the stories that comprise your community's heritage is of utmost importance.

Community experiences can be planned to reveal authentic assets and activities with specific customers in mind. Although it has many attributes beyond Cannery Row, John Steinbeck's novels gave Monterey, California tremendous exposure. Monterey Bay Aquarium capitalized on the history of the area by placing their world-class facilities in a former sardine cannery in the heart of Cannery Row. Kayaking among sea otters, whale watching in the bay, and dining at restaurants that cooperate with the aquarium's Seafood Watch program creates a charming experience package – a must-do for residents and visitors alike. Construction walls have Steinbeck era scenes painted on them and gutters are stenciled with reminders that anything dumped in the street ends up in the bay. Steinbeck's stories, local seafood, and interaction with rich marine environments combine to create a unique, authentic experience that brings people back

again and again. Social, economic and environmental interests blend brilliantly in a desirable local lifestyle while providing a world-class tourism experience.

Historic Washington State Park in southwestern Arkansas comprises the quaint community of Washington that celebrates the history of Arkansas in the 1800s. Managed by Arkansas State Parks in conjunction with the Pioneer Washington Restoration Foundation, the 1874 Hempstead County Courthouse serves as the Visitor Center and heritage interpreters conduct programming

Monterey Bay Aquarium anchors the shops that line the Cannery Row historic district of Monterey, California.

authentic to the period. New buildings are required to build in the historic style of the mid-1800s. It is a thoughtfully managed and interpreted community of about 200 residents that draws about 100,000 tourists annually. The care with which the community maintains its historic integrity makes the annual Jonquil Festival seem that much more out of place. Wigs, pet sunglasses, and a variety of other modern, out of context vendors that travel a flea market circuit and are not local citizens dominate the event with only one or two local craftsmen displaying historic crafts scattered among the booths. Visitors can be photographed with live baby tigers or take the kids to slide down an inflatable great white shark. The only jonquils to be seen (which are by no means unique to Washington) are in the parking area. This single event does not characterize the town but because no significant attempt is made to blend the authentic stories of the area into the festival, people come and go without any sense of the community.

Special events can, in fact, provide perfect opportunities to showcase what is unique about a community if authenticity is maintained throughout the event. Collinsville, Illinois, has hosted the International Horseradish Festival for more than two decades. They claim that southern Illinois grows 80% of the horseradish in the world and that the Collinsville area alone grows 60% of the world's annual horseradish crop. They have built a community event around a unique agricultural crop of the region. Similar food festivals have developed in Gilroy, California with the Garlic Festival or Lodi, California with its summer Asparagus Festival and fall Grape Festival. The interesting thing about these events is the focus on the local produce that provides the necessary authenticity for the audience to become completely immersed in the regional culture and plan return visits year after year.

Authenticity is neither easy to determine nor to protect as a community value. In his book, *Lies Across America*, James Loewen points out that historians often disagree about the course of history and that the history that is recorded may or may not reflect reality, either intentionally or unintentionally. It is important that the community identify the value of authentic stories and the real sense of place that has grown out of centuries of history and prehistory to be able to solidify its theme, even if some of those stories are less than flattering. It is perhaps only too human to embrace a dramatic story or recounting of an event that is exaggerated or even untrue, but this is rarely in the best interest of the community over the long term. Each community has its own human history, agricultural story, economic story and ecological identity. Thoughtful civic engagement in the planning process will reveal those unique and authentic stories and the most appropriate ways in which to tell them.

> It is important that the community identify the value of authentic stories and the real sense of place that has grown out of centuries of history and prehistory to be able to solidify its theme, even if some of those stories are less than flattering.

Cantera

PUERTO RICO, USA

You might visit San Juan, Puerto Rico, and not hear of Cantera community. It's buried in the obscurity of being lower income housing, away from the beaten path among the beaches and European atmosphere of Condado. But Cantera is home to fishermen, working people and many unemployed. The community is on a peninsula of land mostly surrounded by Laguna San Jose, a very large brackish water lake between San Juan and Carolina, the most urban part of Puerto Rico.

We took a unique tour with a Cantera boat captain from their commercial fishing boat dock located on San Jose Lagoon. For almost four hours we traveled along the lagoon's lush edges of black, white and red mangroves. Great egrets, snowy egrets, green herons, great blue herons and reddish egrets posed in the mangroves as we moved slowly down the Suaréz Canal that connects Laguna San Jose with Laguna Torrecillas. We saw dozens of large iguanas draped on the trees and several swimming along the edge of the canal. We learned that large tarpon of six feet length are common to the lagoons and a big attraction for fishermen.

The working class community of Cantera in San Juan, Puerto Rico, nestles among high-rise hotels and the estates of wealthy people from all over the world.

As we went through a highway underpass we saw a fisherman's camp and several men casting purse nets, while some fished from the bank with poles. In Torrecillas Lagoon, we passed the homes of the rich and famous people who can afford waterfront property and noted the disappearance of the mangrove forests where houses have been built. Along the way we saw the nests of common moorhens nestled on the end of fragile branches over the water where predators dare not go. Ospreys hunted overhead and one perched on a limb with a fish in its talons. Pelicans, frigate birds, tern and skimmers flew overhead or perched along the mangroves.

Finally we reached a small village near the opening to the Atlantic Ocean and we stopped to drink fish soup and enjoy a Medalla Lite Beer. The cafe manager showed us the fresh red snapper and mahi mahi (dorado) filling their freezers. They buy local fish daily directly from fishermen and then resell to restauranteurs or individuals. After we got back on the boat, we took a quick sortie out into the Atlantic near Pinoñes State Forest and then turned back into the lagoon to cruise back to the Cantera community. It was a beautiful tour and intriguing look at the natural and cultural heritage of Puerto Rico we would never have found on our own. That evening we sat in an outdoor café at Piñones enjoying local food and watching people swim in the shallows of the Atlantic beaches just below us.

Fernando Silva, Executive Director of INCICO (Institute for the Conservation of Puerto Rico) and Eliezer Nieves, a Certified Interpretive Trainer with National Association for Interpretation (NAI) and Santa Ana Nature Center Director showed us this evolving program in San Juan. They are helping community leaders in Cantera employ interpretive planning and guiding techniques in this unique community-based ecotourism program.

Peninsula Expeditions is a project of the Cantera Community, a community corporation working to improve socio-economic conditions locally through development of ecotours and other enterprises that support ecotourism. Driving into the community and to the boat marina we noticed the lagoon or lake edge had many animal pens, stored recreational equipment, boats, gardens and picnic tables. People leave their apartment houses to enjoy some of the countryside amenities of having chickens or rabbits and a small garden. Many of them once lived in rural areas and came to the city for opportunities that didn't happen as hoped.

The experience that we enjoyed is available to tourists, cruise boat visitors and local people. Local young people will initially be trained as interpretive guides and eventually as NAI Certified Interpretive Guides. Fernando and Eliezer told us about the past year and a half of meeting with community leaders to listen and discuss what they might do collaboratively. They launched this new tourist initiative using a pontoon boat purchased to provide tours. Early conversations with local fishermen led to development of a resource map. Their knowledge of the area from fishing is so detailed that they can map the floor of the lake almost exactly from memory. The resulting map served as a resource for planning natural and cultural history tours.

This kind of collaboration between INCICO, a nonprofit organization with conservation and interpretation expertise, and the Cantera community is becoming more common around the world. Ecotourism offers opportunities for people to make a living by providing transportation, food, housing and guide services as they share their communities with people who enjoy learning

Fernando Silva (left) and Eliezer Nieves (right) work with local fishermen to develop a boat tour that will bring San Juan visitors to the wildlife-rich shores of the lagoons.

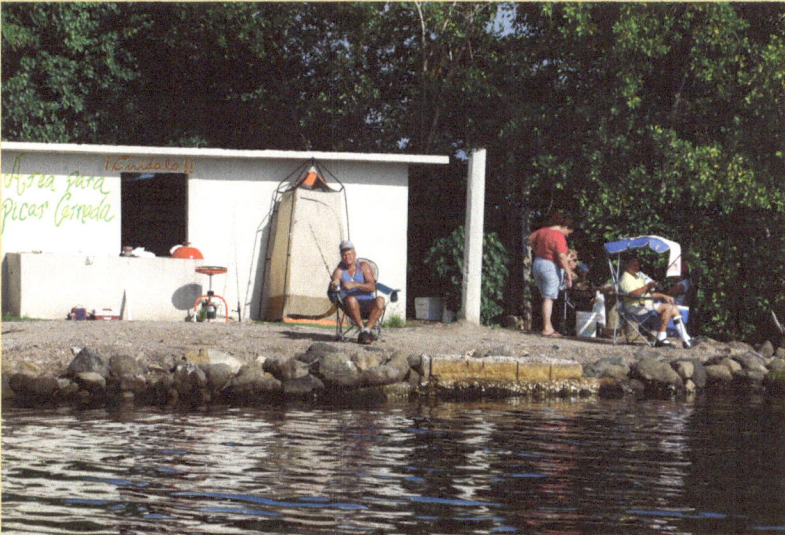

Local people rely on the lagoons for food and recreation.

Visitors get better views of wildlife, like the yellow-crowned night heron, from a water-based tour.

Anglers using purse nets are commonly seen along the canals interconnecting the lagoons.

about other people and places. INCICO plays a key role as facilitator in Puerto Rico. Cantera Corporation is developing an exciting project for the local community and should create a rich opportunity for local residents and tourists to San Juan to escape for the day into a rich ecosystem with fascinating cultural and natural history stories to share. Planning with community leaders takes time but can result in sustainable development that allows community citizens to work in ways they understand.

—Tim Merriman

Photo Essay

Historic Washington State Park and its surrounding community host an annual Jonquil Festival.

The local resident broom maker and Mennonite food stand seem appropriate to the unique historic community but tend to get lost among the other vendors.

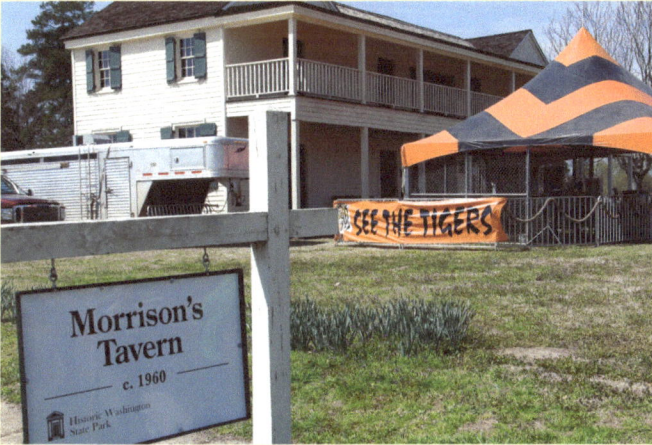

The construction of Morrison Tavern matches the historic buildings from a century before. Unfortunately, the thoughtful attempt at construction is somewhat masked by a baby tiger photo opportunity that does not match the historic theme of the site.

Access to the Visitor Center housed in the historic courthouse is almost obscured by the event booths.

Great White Sharks? In Arkansas?

Medieval homes and buildings punctuate the picturesque Tuscan landscape.

The narrow streets of San Quirico in the World Heritage Landscape of Val d'Orcia encourage walking throughout the community.

Tuscany is known for incredible landscapes filled with olive groves, vineyards and yellow safflower fields. Local farmers often open their homes as part of the agriturismo movement that encourages bed and breakfast experiences on working farms.

Local cheeses, olive oil and wine can be tried in shops, enjoyed in cafes or packaged to go home with residents or tourists.

Cafés in Tuscany serve as traditional meeting places for young and old with no pressure to move along.

The freshness and exquisite taste of Italian dishes speaks to the use of locally-grown and produced food.

Working Together on a Growing Dream

PUEBLO, COLORADO, USA

In the early 1980s, Pueblo plunged into a deep economic downturn. Colorado Fuel & Iron, a steel company, downsized and thousands of people lost their jobs. Pueblo Army Depot closed, eliminating about 5,000 jobs. Unemployment approached 20% and it seemed like very dark days for one of the oldest communities in the state, a community that was a burgeoning western town well before Denver existed.

The Arkansas and Fountain Rivers flow through this city of 100,000 and converge on the southeast corner of the downtown. Both had become dumping grounds for many people in the city. Large appliances, tires and debris were common on the banks of the rivers. In1981, the two-year old Pueblo Nature Center began holding annual river cleanups. In a matter of a few years the big stuff was gone from the river corridors and the annual event focused on smaller and smaller items to remove. Pride was growing slowly. People began to see their rivers as important assets, not just flood threats as in the past. Newly built bicycle trails were installed in parts of both river corridors but they didn't connect.

The Historic Arkansas River Project (HARP) in Pueblo, Colorado, brought a hidden water channel back to the surface as a beautiful downtown amenity.

Necessity really does seem to be the mother of invention. A number of good things began to happen due to thoughtful leadership and collaboration on a variety of fronts. The Greenway Foundation and Nature Center merged to become The Greenway and Nature Center of Pueblo. Pueblo Conservancy District, formed in the 1920s in response to a disastrous flood to manage levees and property along the Arkansas River, called other community planners and resource representatives together for a breakfast. The Greenway and Nature Center, Colorado State Parks, Colorado Division of Wildlife, City Planning, County Planning, City Parks, and Trout Unlimited all sent representatives. The discussion centered on how to improve the river corridors with virtually no local resources available. The Conservancy could invest some funds annually on maintenance roads along the river, but their mandate was not public recreation.

The monthly breakfasts became a routine and the group began landing hundreds of thousands of dollars in grants and donations from Fishing is Fun (Dingle-Johnson monies), state trails grants, private foundations and

Public art and program space along HARP bring people downtown to enjoy the historic neighborhoods that were once blighted areas to be avoided.

individual donors. A foundation grant funded a needed bridge to cross the Arkansas River and an U.S. Army Corps of Engineers project built a bridge needed over the Fountain. The disjunct Greenway was suddenly a 26-mile network throughout the community, extending to Lake Pueblo. The nature center organized volunteer trail rangers. The Conservancy continued to do maintenance projects in the river bottoms that provided matching funds to help land recreational and river access grants.

One meeting brought up the opportunity to look at what other river communities had done to make their rivers a more important economic development and community asset. Representatives from most of the breakfast planning coalition took a trip to San Antonio for a cook's tour of the famed Riverwalk and then on to Wichita, Kansas, to see their very attractive trails and amenities along the Arkansas River. All were impressed by the insider's look at these communities who had made their river heritage an important central story in community development. This trip provided ideas for everyone about what might be done in Pueblo.

Native animals depicted in small and large sculptures along Pueblo's trails help establish the sense of place and tell the story of local natural areas.

Sidewalk cafes and boutiques along the HARP streets and trails encourage people to stay longer and enjoy the ambiance in this historic community once known primarily for its steel mills.

The Conservancy continued to provide leadership in planning an idea to bring water back to the surface in downtown Pueblo as a controlled amenity. Levees built to protect the area from serious flooding in the 1920s were imposing concrete walled structures that hid the Arkansas River from view through downtown. An old dedicated underground water culvert for a power plant was buried beneath the city streets.

Funds to complete this major water project were the limiting factor. It would take millions to bring visible waterways into the historic downtown in Pueblo. A bond issue to raise the funds was presented to taxpayers and they voted to approve it. The Historic Arkansas River Project (HARP) became a reality in 1995. The project is about to enter Phase Three of development and has attracted a convention center, new hotels, restaurants and many shops nearby while bringing more diverse commerce to the historic downtown that was once a blighted area and an eyesore for visitors to Pueblo.

Many factors went into this effort but the breakfast planning and collaboration meetings were key in the very early stages. No single entity could have done very much alone. Sharing the responsibilities for grants writing, heavy equipment, landscape plans, engineering and fundraising contributed to steady progress that has turned the river corridors into important amenities for special events, daily walks by local people and field outings by school children. The visit by the planning team to San Antonio and Wichita was also important in helping everyone have a larger vision for what could happen. The rich sense of place that the rivers provide are an important part of the identity of this unique western community. The developments have been tasteful and thematic in preserving the old West feeling of the historic downtown area. Pride in these accomplishments is evident among the many participants who made it all happen.

—Tim Merriman

5   **Rewarding**

Holistic, appropriate community experiences that create emotional and intellectual connections deliver **rewards**. Rewards can be monetary or they can manifest in improved quality of life, stronger relationships, preservation of culture, or a healthier environment. Essentially, rewards should reflect the combined triple bottom line of social, economic, and environmental results, rather than focusing on any one of those elements to the detriment of the others. Desired rewards must be determined by a common vision, goals, and objectives that identify measures of success based on a process that involves diverse stakeholders in a collaborative planning environment.

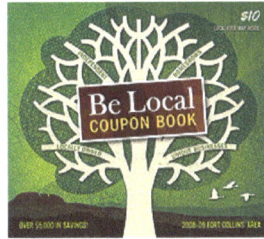

The Be Local Coupon Book in Fort Collins, Colorado, offers a chance to track success through numbers of redeemed coupons.

Using logic models to frame success

One of the simpler methods for determining what rewards are appropriate for your community is to develop a logic model. Logic models create a series of if-then statements that provide a framework for establishing short-term actions that lead to long-term benefits. Although there are many different

Logic Model Diagram

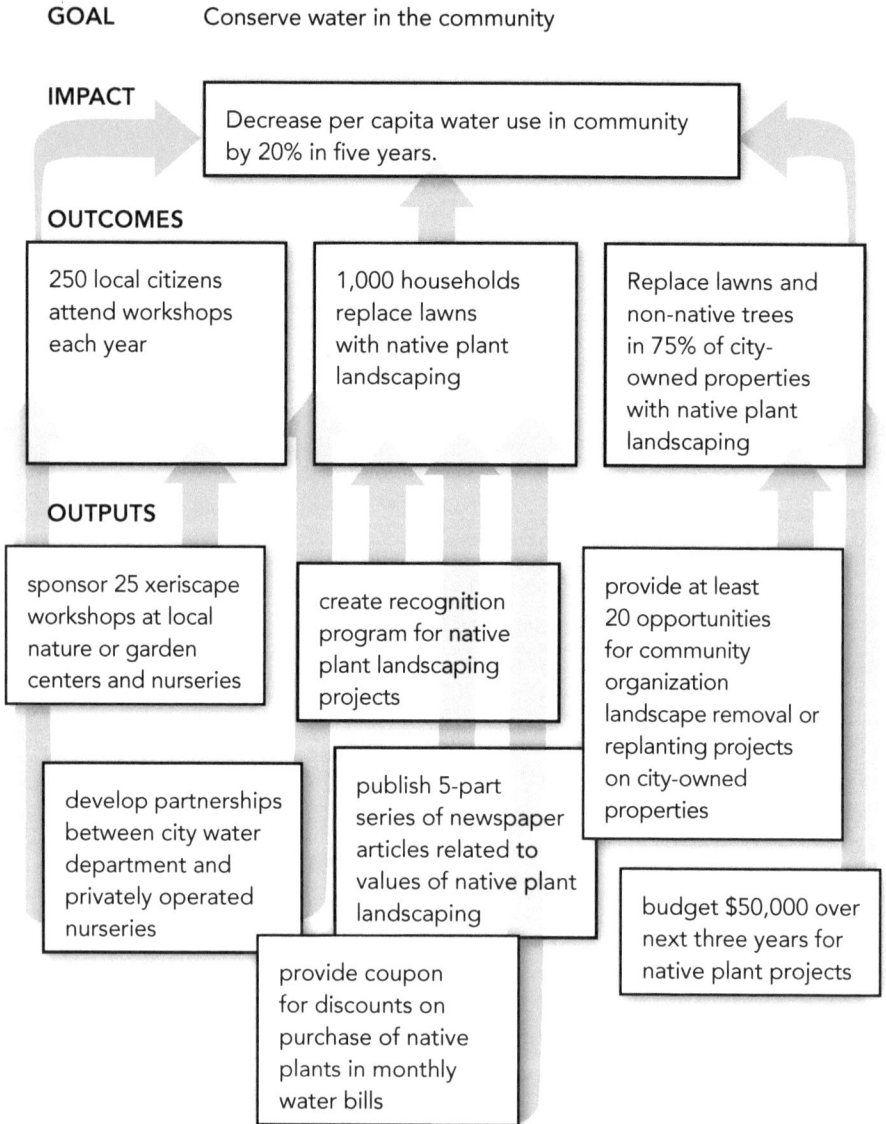

GOAL   Conserve water in the community

IMPACT

> Decrease per capita water use in community by 20% in five years.

OUTCOMES

250 local citizens attend workshops each year	1,000 households replace lawns with native plant landscaping	Replace lawns and non-native trees in 75% of city-owned properties with native plant landscaping

OUTPUTS

sponsor 25 xeriscape workshops at local nature or garden centers and nurseries

create recognition program for native plant landscaping projects

provide at least 20 opportunities for community organization landscape removal or replanting projects on city-owned properties

develop partnerships between city water department and privately operated nurseries

publish 5-part series of newspaper articles related to values of native plant landscaping

budget $50,000 over next three years for native plant projects

provide coupon for discounts on purchase of native plants in monthly water bills approaches to writing a logic model that vary slightly on terminology, the basic premise remains the same: outputs (what the community does) lead to outcomes (behaviors of residents and visitors) that lead to impacts (benefits to the community). A logic model approach allows planners to think about desired long-term results and then think backwards to determine what has to happen to achieve those results, rather than focusing solely on the resources at hand or short-term activities that may not serve a greater purpose.

Each of the logic model components should be framed as a measurable objective. Many organizations have worked in the realm of output objectives as a reporting measure – x number of pamphlets printed; x number of special events held; x number of visitors through the visitor center. The only problem with thinking solely in terms of output objectives is that there is no bigger picture being considered. The numbers may reveal what you've accomplished, but they don't suggest whether what you've accomplished has had any significant effect on the well-being of the organization, the resource, or the community. If, on the other hand, you can show a direct link between the activities or products you offer and changes in behavior or attitudes as a result of participation in those activities, you can demonstrate that your activity offerings are productive and worthy of the resources they consume.

> If you can show a direct link between the activities or products you offer and changes in behavior or attitudes as a result of participation in those activities, you can demonstrate that your activity offerings are productive and worthy of the resources they consume.

Outcome objectives identify the specific behaviors that are expected as a result of interaction with the outputs. So for example, if an output objective is to hold a quarterly special event that provides a variety of experience packages with each event, one outcome objective might be to establish a specific number of collaborative partnerships between experience providers.

Another might be to identify a specific number of repeat participants in those events. An impact objective might be the amount of money brought into the town by the events. It could also be a shared incentive plan that would directly benefit the collaborating partners as well as the community as a whole, or the number of local jobs created by those events.

It's important to note that while there may be a one-to-one relationship between outputs, outcomes, and impacts, it's more likely that it will take several outputs to achieve two or three specified outcomes that will lead to a single impact. There is no magic formula to determine how many objectives at each level are required for success. Each logic model must be written to express the unique needs of the planning community and will therefore, look uniquely different from all others.

The true beauty of a logic model is that it serves a dual function. As a planning tool, it helps to frame the decisions you will make regarding the allocation of resources toward achieving desired results. As an evaluation tool, it can be used to review progress in-stream or at the end of a specified time period. Consequently, the evaluative measures must be reasonable both in terms of expectations and the methods used to measure results so that the rewards of your community experience planning efforts are evident.

6 Thematic

Communities that deliver appropriate and rewarding experiences usually find that they connect with residents and visitors emotionally with a simple, straightforward **theme**. Thematic communication is not a new idea – it dates back to the ancient Greeks and the first organized plays. Simply put, a theme is the message that you want people to understand about your community. It sums up your community's core values and the significant stories that contribute to its sense of place in a single sentence. A well-designed theme helps the diverse interests in your community find common ground, allowing everyone to work together to project a unified message about what makes your community unique.

Joseph Pine and James Gilmore (*Experience Economy*, 2000) talk about the importance of thematic presentation in the experience economy that comprises successful businesses today. In an architectural context, a theme is often just a harmonious collection of colors and textures without any real message. Certainly, architectural elements help convey a central message, but it's important to look beyond the façades to the real, rich stories that create sense of place if you want to build those emotional and intellectual connections in a holistic manner and create meaningful, lasting, and rewarding experiences. Sam Ham's 2007 research on achieving conservation objectives through heritage interpretation indicates that "by communicating themes and providing experiential learning, you are planting seeds (beliefs) that can ultimately influence (reinforce or change) how people think, feel and behave."

Ham states that people remember themes, but tend to forget individual facts (*Environmental Interpretation*, 1992). This belief is borne out by William Thorndyke's 1979 research that tested what people remember from a presentation. Thorndyke found that an organized litany of facts was no more effective in retention of information than a jumbled litany of facts. Organizing information has the value of allowing people to pay attention according to David Ausubel (1960), but organization alone does not deliver memorable messages. Thorndyke did find that thematic communication was more effective than a non-thematic presentation in helping people understand and recall general content. The theme delivers what Ausubel calls an "advance organizer." It lets people know what the experience or presentation is about and they are more likely to stay engaged and leave with their own understanding of the theme or belief.

The implications of this research for communities are important. Clearly, the tendency of tour guides, chamber of commerce websites, and other information systems to focus on an interminable list of facts instead of a more complete message ensures that there will be no sense of place and therefore no connections to your community. A theme, on the other hand, helps people think more holistically about the community and remember the message. But how does a community with a variety of stories to tell settle on a single theme? Does this mean that some stories don't get told?

In 1954 George Miller's *Magic Number Seven Plus or Minus Two* research suggested that most people can carry seven chunks of information or ideas about a new topic and almost everyone can handle at least five chunks. More recent research by Cowan (2000) suggests that the upper limit is four chunks of information. Miller and Cowan's chunk theories encourage the notion that if there is one central message or theme driving communication strategies, it might be possible to group stories with common elements into subthemes that support the central theme.

Hangzhou in Zhejiang Province of eastern China is a great example of a city planned around a central theme. It has been a center of commerce

Theme, Subtheme, Storyline Diagram

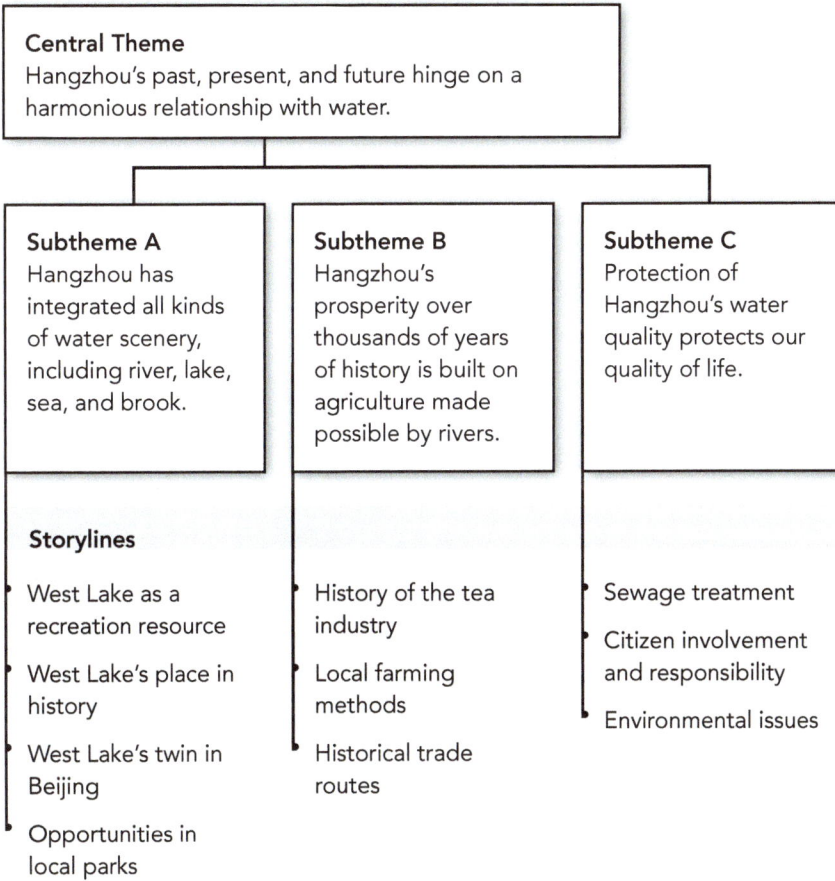

Central Theme
Hangzhou's past, present, and future hinge on a
harmonious relationship with water.

Subtheme A
Hangzhou has
integrated all kinds
of water scenery,
including river, lake,
sea, and brook.

Subtheme B
Hangzhou's
prosperity over
thousands of years
of history is built on
agriculture made
possible by rivers.

Subtheme C
Protection of
Hangzhou's water
quality protects our
quality of life.

Storylines

West Lake as a
recreation resource

West Lake's place in
history

West Lake's twin in
Beijing

Opportunities in
local parks

History of the tea
industry

Local farming
methods

Historical trade
routes

Sewage treatment

Citizen involvement
and responsibility

Environmental issues

for 5,000 or more years but rose to fame as the capital of the Song Dynasty
in 1123. It is estimated that more than two million people lived there even
at that time. A focal point of the city is West Lake, a beautiful natural lake
in the Yangtze River Valley that so impressed the empress of China she had
a mirror image of it constructed as the setting for the spectacular Summer
Palace in Beijing. Marco Polo, the Venetian explorer, described it as the most
beautiful city in the world. It has had a strong sense of place for a very long

Hangzhou, China, has been famous for its natural scenery, especially West Lake, for more than 1,000 years. Once the capital of China during the Song Dynasty, the city is home to almost four million people.

time, wrapped around its history with plentiful water resources. Today, the local government is committed to protecting that rich cultural and natural history and identity.

A booklet distributed by the Hangzhou government clearly relates Hangzhou's central theme – water and people are in perfect harmony in Hangzhou. Subthemes, which are developed throughout the city and its environs at a number of sites, help tell the stories of how Hangzhou protected and valued its water resources in the past and how it continues to do so today.

At Hangzhou's National Tea Museum, calligraphic representations of the symbol for tea are embedded in the entry path and water-based entry feature. Exhibits focus on the history of the tea industry. Program activities include a tea ceremony and guided tours through terraces of tea plants. The gift shop offers loose and packaged green tea, teapots, and other related items. The water feature that winds throughout the grounds is a constant reminder of the central theme of the museum: without water, there is no tea. This relationship of water to agriculture is one important subtheme that plays out in a number of places.

Xixi Wetlands is a national sanctuary and museum that tells the story of how water shaped the lives of local people in the Hangzhou area.

Xixi Wetlands on the outskirts of Hangzhou is an attraction developed around a series of wetlands that have served for centuries as a place for people to live off the land and water. The myriad canals offer the opportunity to view the wetlands from a boat, with footpaths connecting the land bases. Mulberry trees are grown along some canals allowing silkworms to feast on the mulberry leaves, and then enrich the water for fish farming with their droppings. The entire process of harvesting silkworms and turning the silk into thread and then into a finished product is documented through exhibits that encourage interaction. Silk embroidery artists demonstrate how they create the beautiful pictures available in shops throughout the site.

To help address the subtheme of water quality, Hangzhou city officials sponsor a water symposium that brings experts from all over the world to investigate issues associated with water quality and sustainable tourism based on water resources. The urban sewage treatment plant releases water back into the community in a wetland that serves as a beautiful and well-used public park. The operator proudly shows off the water treatment system and testing

The National Tea Museum in Hangzhou makes it clear that without water there is no tea. Tea villages bring people into rural areas to enjoy the scenery, local tea and a chance to play games and visit with friends.

This wetland park within Hangzhou is a popular place to walk and see water lilies but it is also where treated sewage water is returned to the watershed as clean as drinking water.

Hangzhou sponsors a "water scenery" conference that helps establish their brand as a unique place with natural scenery while bringing them the most current technologies and understanding of water resources.

lab, even offering to drink the treated water to demonstrate its purity.

The beauty of West Lake and other city parks that include natural or constructed water features relate to the subtheme of how the aesthetics of water are an important part of life and help to create community gathering places. Each of these three subthemes incorporate multiple interests and experiences, but more importantly, they each support the central theme that the harmony of life in Hangzhou is dependent on good care of water resources. Evident throughout the city is the need for all people to be stewards of this important resource that helps define Hangzhou. These experiences fit together in a holistic tapestry reflective of the history of the community and the unique, authentic resources of the area. They relate to the universal concepts of life, beauty, and health, helping people connect to the community emotionally as well as intellectually. And the rewards are evident – a thriving city that still relies on its water resources for its economic, social, and environmental well-being.

The Heart of Santa Clara La Laguna

GUATEMALA

Guatemala faces chronic poverty and unemployment, high rates of child malnutrition and illiteracy, rising gang violence and ever increasing environmental and cultural degradation. Concurrently, Guatemala is rich in culture, with 23 distinct languages, pleasant climate, world-renowned coffee; the country attracts a steady stream of international tourism.

The Refuge Interpretive Trail resulted from a ten-month interpretive consultancy in several towns around Lake Atitlan. With its stunning views, the lake is the country's second most visited tourist site behind the colonial city, Antigua and in front of the Tikal ruins. The trail is more than a nice walk in the woods; it is a story that engages the body, the heart and the mind. It reflects the history and values of the Maya K'iche' community of Santa Clara La Laguna. The trail is set in the Highlands of Guatemala in a mountainous cloud forest in Chuiraxamolo' Municipal Ecological Park, a protected area managed by the Santa Clara La Laguna, Sololá, Guatemala, Central America. Established in 2004, the park helps to conserve the natural and cultural patrimony of the region, promoting community ecotourism and environmental education.

Traditions like the town fair thrive in Santa Clara La Laguna, a Maya K'iche' town in the Highlands of Guatemala.

I worked on behalf of Vivamos Mejor (roughly translated to "that we might live better"), a non-profit organization working with communities around Lake Atitlan. Besides sectors of health and reforestation, their ecotourism branch concentrates on community based tourism. Their mission is to help reduce poverty in the towns around the lake through sustainable development. The goal is to contribute to a better quality of life for the indigenous communities around the lake through promotion, sustainable development and community self-management.

The participatory process featured community meetings to talk about interpretation, tourism, and planning. In these meetings, we determined that municipal parks have good potential for sustainable development, but this depends on two things: that what is being visited isn't eroded or degraded to the point of rendering it inauthentic or uninteresting; and that local people protect and preserve the natural and cultural recourses that have sustained them through feast and famine.

Later we tried something innovative—creativity workshops that included

93

Village elders were the guests of honor at the trail inauguration.

Depicting local residents in the artwork created strong connections to the project.

park staff, community elders and leaders, artisans and members of an organic coffee cooperative. The goal of the workshops was to open the minds of the participants to their own creativity and the significances of their culture and place. The workshops resulted in the identification of many of Santa Clara's outstanding tangible and intangible attributes that led to a determination of the theme for the trail. With four Maya altars that now are shared by Catholic and Evangelical groups, the park symbolizes religious tolerance and spiritual refuge. The park is also provides habitat for scores of plant, animal and bird species. Habitat was linked to the universal idea of home and protection from extraction, hunting and encroachment. A portion of the trail was once the old road that local people used to carry goods to and from market. Upon reaching the mountaintop, they would put down their packs and rest for a while. Rest and renovation and escape from modernity or towns and

René Dionisio, the project's art director, working on his bamboo kiosk design.

cities are other forms of refuge. Finally, during the protracted Guatemalan Civil War (1960- 1996), many indigenous families were forced from their homes. They escaped the military patrols by hiding in the forested mountains. The forest sheltered them and was yet another form of refuge.

René Dionisio, a multi-talented local artist, served as the project's director of art. Throughout the project, I worked with him to teach him interpretive theory and practice and he readily came to understand that the construction and style of the signs and framing were as much a part of the message as the text on the signs. René conceived a kiosk made of bamboo and stone that he called the 'bamboo egg'. In an area that is threatened by deforestation, this unique design promotes bamboo as a renewable construction material.

Peace Corps Volunteers participated in every phase of the project.

The Refuge Trail offers insight and inspiration to local and international visitors.

Bamboo is more flexible than steel, produces 30% more oxygen than trees, grows rapidly and is an intelligent alternative to using wood for construction.

René, along with another local artist, Manuel Chavajay, painted the sign images. This added to the sense of place and furthered their professional development. Eny Roland Hernández, an aspiring professional photographer was hired to photograph the park, the town and community members in traditional dress to inform the artwork. The artists promoted a sense of local pride, ownership and relevance by depiction of several residents of Santa Clara La Laguna in the sign art.

Vivamos Mejor seeks to help municipalities better manage their natural resources and take advantage of opportunities for community based tourism as a way to alleviate chronic poverty, but the completion of this project was never guaranteed. Vivamos Mejor invested in the interpretive planning and trail design but left the financing of trail construction in the hands of the municipal council. The mayor of Santa Clara La Laguna is Anastasio Ajuc is a former school teacher and really grasped the importance of a project that tried to capture and present the best values of his culture. The members of the council saw value in educating and inspiring visitors about Santa Clara, the K'iche' culture, and the rational use of natural resources. They approved the cost of trail construction. The economic benefits of the project were spread throughout the community. Restaurants, hardware stores, artisans and laborers received direct economic benefits from the project.

Community based interpretive planning isn't for everyone. You have to love what you do. Heart comes from caring about every detail and working as hard as you can with what you have. Heart comes from having a good cause and giving people the opportunity to contribute. I would estimate that over one hundred community members contributed to this project in one way or another. In the grand scheme it's not much, but one time in the Highlands of Guatemala, one hundred beating hearts worked together to build a trail.

—Chris Mayer, Ph.D., Interpretive Planner

Mystic Seaport in Connecticut maintains a strong sense of place through diverse attractions.

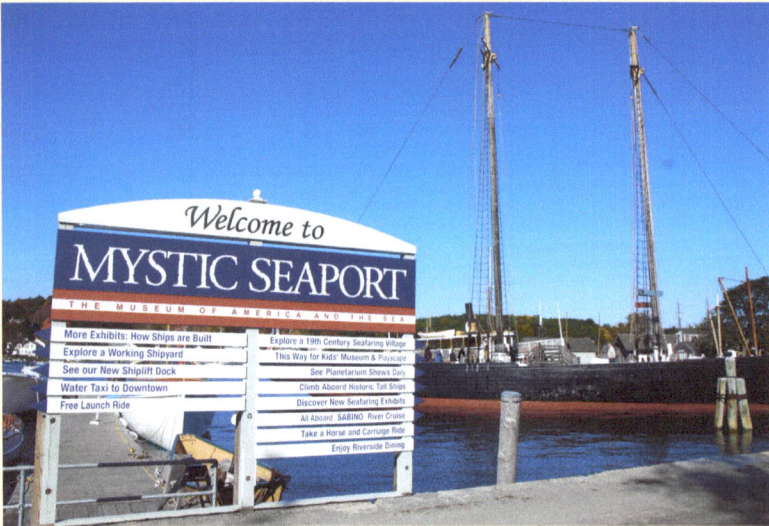

The welcome sign at Mystic Seaport invites guests to explore the community in a variety of ways.

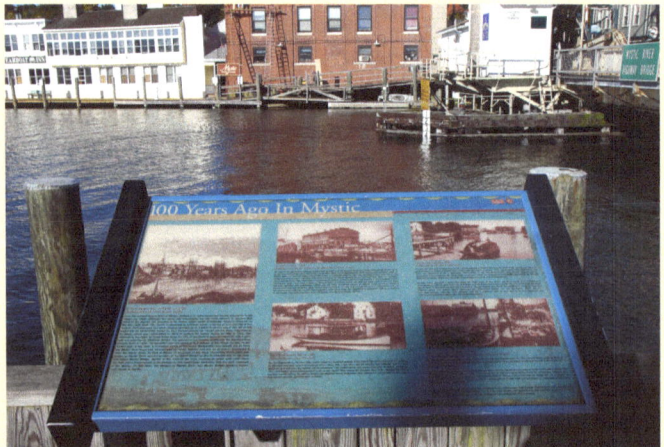

Waterfront interpretive signs help guests see how the community values their rich boat-building and seaport history.

Mystic Aquarium connects residents and visitors to ocean fish and wildlife in the local area.

The Mystic Seaport Museum uses living history to tell the story of ship-building in the community over hundreds of years.

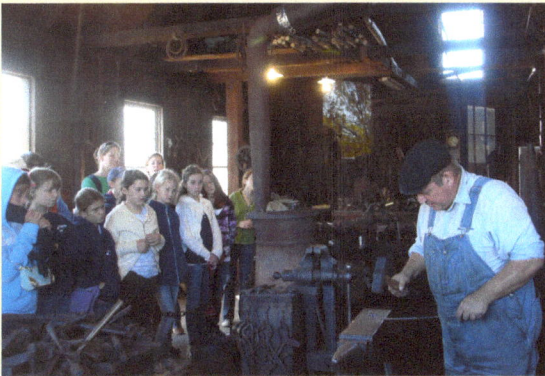

Children enjoy seeing craftspeople such as this blacksmith making typical items used on a ship.

7 Creating Your Own Community Experience Plan

Although every community must approach a planning process somewhat differently based on the unique structure and interests of the community, taking some basic steps will help to ensure that the process goes smoothly and that all interests are fairly represented. Some general parameters to keep in mind as you work through the process:

Don't expect to copy the success of others. One of the challenges for a heritage-based community is the tendency of leaders and entrepreneurs to want to copy another seemingly successful community. It's easy to get caught up in the excitement of something that looks interesting. Let's do an air show! We need a race track! We'll start a film festival! How about an IMAX theatre? These kinds of choices, unless based on sound planning that indicates a chance of success, usually do not build on the strength of the community and may or may not work financially. Just because they work in one place doesn't mean they'll work in another. Furthermore, they do not strengthen the sense of place unless they arise from some authentic value of the community.

Find incentives for the positive changes desired in the community. Fort Collins, Colorado, formed a Downtown Development Authority that uses tax-increment funding to give incentive grants to local business owners in the Old Town District if they build a façade that matches the general architectural theme of the community. Some communities pass planning and zoning ordinances that require franchise stores to build and put up signs to match the architectural themes. Once you know what changes you would like to see, devise a reward system that works for your community to encourage voluntary compliance and further development of creative ideas that will lead to desired changes.

Collaboration among businesses should be encouraged. Businesses have a natural inclination to compete but collaboration is often necessary to create a successful community for all. Collaboration can include cross-promotion of each other's businesses or packaging of services to create total experiences. Local business owners might also work together to train front-line staff as interpretive hosts who help guests understand and connect with community resources. Directors of heritage attractions such as museums, zoos, nature centers, parks and historic sites should meet regularly amongst themselves and with other leaders in the community to share ideas for funding and other joint projects that benefit all.

Plan before investing. One of the great challenges in any community is to take the time to plan thoughtfully and develop specific objectives to be met before investing precious grant funds or public funding in media such as signs, promotions, or other tourism aids or public facilities. If the investment is ineffective because the wrong media or facility decisions are being made, the money is wasted. An influential person or donor may want the money spent in a specific way and often it is unavoidable to do it differently, but a plan pays for itself very quickly by targeting the investment strategically to meet specific objectives. The following steps will help you get started in the planning process.

Step 1 - Assessment

Every community has strengths and weaknesses. Identifying them through an assessment process will help you capitalize on the strengths and work toward improving or eliminating weaknesses.

Who should perform the assessment?

No one knows your community as well as the people who live there. Unfortunately, the people who live and work in a community may also have a strong personal investment that keeps them from being completely objective in assessing strengths and weaknesses. It may be necessary to bring in an outside opinion to review and analyze a situation, but that analysis must also consider the viewpoints of residents. One process that might be useful would be to create a self-assessment tool that could be circulated among residents, then provide the collected information to a consulting facilitator who can review the information and lead a focus group of residents through a process to achieve consensus on strengths and weaknesses.

What should we be assessing?

To be truly effective, a self-assessment tool should be created for each community's unique situation rather than using a template and expecting it to fit every situation. Many communities use the simple SWOT method, listing their strengths, weaknesses, opportunities and threats or barriers to success. While there is value in this approach, it could be augmented by looking specifically at the elements of the HEART model to keep the discussion focused on how to put and keep the heart of your community intact. Here a few suggestions to get you started in assessing the strengths, weaknesses and opportunities in your community.

Holistic?

1. *Determine the extent of the community.* Does your community consist of a single city, a zone or neighborhood within a city, multiple cities within a region, or a linear string of cities or other attractions (like a scenic byway)? Although each of these options presents unique challenges, they can all be looked at holistically to create complete experiences.

This community kitchen in Shibakawa, Japan, serves as a place for local women to teach others how to make soba noodles, tofu and other traditional food by hand. School children and visiting adults enjoy the unique chance to learn these techniques and then enjoy the food they prepare in a typical meal.

2. *Apply the visitor experience model.* Once the extent of your community is known, begin to look critically at how people experience it. This step helps you assess the current conditions of your community so that you can begin to plan for necessary improvements. Use a focus group of first-time visitors and a focus group of long-time residents to get multiple perspectives as you walk through each of the five phases of the visitor experience model and look for the strengths and weaknesses in each.

3. *Check for design balance.* Generally speaking, do buildings blend with the landscape? Do they blend with each other? Is there any sense of continuity between old and new? What message comes through from the design elements? Is it the message you want to be sending? Use your focus groups again to help maintain objectivity as you visually assess your community.

Engaging?

1. *Look at your community's website and written promotional materials.* For many tourist destinations the Internet is becoming the most important point of contact. Modern travelers go there first to determine what to do, where to stay, what is affordable and to get a sense of the place. A website is an opportunity to begin establishing connections to your community. Many communities use the website as an information center only rather than a communication opportunity. Rarely does the site identify more than a data bank of motels, restaurants, and attractions. Can you imagine seeing an ad for a movie or a movie trailer that simply said, "Three important stars, a cast of hundreds, set in Cairo, cost eighty million dollars. Don't miss it." Would you go to that movie? Or would you be more intrigued by one that flashes the words "Adventure," "Life," "Death," Survival" on the screen in between short visual clips that evoke a visceral response? Hollywood is masterful at teasing us into wanting to know more by playing on our emotions. Communities can do that as well, but it is vital to be accurate and authentic. Do your website and other written promotional materials reflect the core values of your community or are they simply laundry lists of things to do?

2. *Look around town at signs, local businesses and gathering places.* Do these serve as visual connectors to your community or could they represent any generic location? Can you find any evidence of an attempt at making emotional connections using intangible ideas or universal concepts?

3. *Ask yourself and others what word comes to mind when you think of your community.* This single activity may be the most telling thing you can do during the assessment process because it can quickly reveal whether people are connected to your community or not. If it's hard to come up with a word or if that word is focused on something that is not reflected in the community's core values, then you have just found something that needs work.

Appropriate?

1. *Describe the attributes of existing and potential audiences (both residential and visitor).* Are there specific audiences you would like to make connections with that are underserved in your community? Do you want more or fewer of certain types of audiences? Do you need to rethink what constitutes the "busy season?" What are the expectations, needs, and desires of the various audiences you've described?

2. *Review the authenticity of the experiences currently offered in your community.* Are the local stories true and told accurately or do urban myths proliferate? In some cases, an urban myth has become a community's claim to fame. Take Rhinelander, Wisconsin with its infamous "hodag," a made-up creature that is celebrated by the locals. Though it does not exist, the town has capitalized on the inauthenticity of the animal as its authentic story. This can be taken to a dangerous extreme – in *Lies Across America*, James Loewen describes a town that has built its culture around a "massacre" by local Native Americans. The massacre actually resulted in the killing of one cow, but has created discord for over a century because of how it has been interpreted by the town.

Rewarding?

1. *Visit a few attractions and businesses around your town to determine what rewards are being offered to residents and visitors.* Rewards may come in many forms, but what you're looking for is what would make someone want to come back? Do businesses offer incentives? Is their staff well-trained and hospitable? Are attractions appealing and affordable? Do people feel welcomed everywhere they go?

2. *Identify the things that make it rewarding to live and work in your community.* What parameters are used to determine quality of life? These may become the basis for determining your community's core values. If you are unsure what makes your community rewarding, list the things you wish were happening to stimulate a discussion about how to achieve a more rewarding place to live, work, or visit. This list may then become a series of benchmarks for determining specific objectives to work toward.

A community hula class in Kona-Kailua on the Big Island of Hawaii is one of many that keep alive this dance tradition of the Hawaiian Islands.

Thematic?

1. *After looking at the other components of the* HEART *model as outlined above, identify the primary message you think your community is sending about itself.* Is this the message you want to be sending? What are the important stories that could contribute to creating a more holistic view of your community? Do these stories group naturally into subthemes that might form the basis for some experience packages?

How do we collect the information?

Most communities begin this sort of process with the designation of a steering committee, chaired by a representative of an agency or organization that has the ability to ensure that the process takes place in a timely manner with adequate funding. The steering committee should include representatives of the varied interests in a community: business people (small and large scale businesses), nonprofit organizations, heritage attractions (museums, parks, zoos, etc.), tourism venues, governmental agencies, and the public at large. It can be easy to become overwhelmed by the number of people who might need to be involved, but it is recommended that the steering committee be held to under two dozen people. These people, in turn, can identify other individuals and groups that should be brought into the process through focus groups, surveys, or public input meetings.

If a good facilitator is not part of the steering committee, it may be necessary to hire a facilitator to keep meetings moving along productively and ensure that deadlines are met. Don't assume the chair of the steering committee will facilitate the process. If a facilitator is brought in, the chair of the committee should be the primary contact for the facilitator so that communication is clear and appropriate throughout the process; otherwise, one individual with specific interests on the larger committee may attempt to push the group to support only his or her own interest.

At the first meeting of the steering committee, the facilitator should work with the group to establish a process for assessment that everyone can support. Maybe small subgroups of the committee will look at specific elements of the HEART model and then report back on their findings to the larger group for discussion and decision-making. Or you might want to send out a SWOT survey form to the community at large and then filter the information collected with the steering committee's findings.

The most important thing to keep in mind is that the entire community must be engaged in the process (not necessarily every individual, but certainly representatives of the varied interests). Without a commitment to civic engagement in the planning process, the chances of achieving success are limited.

The assessment process should move forward on the time schedule that is appropriate for the community. It may take a week, a month, or a year to adequately assess the community's strengths, weaknesses, and desires for future development. Obviously, the larger the community, and the larger the steering committee, the more complex and longer the assessment phase is likely to be.

What do we do with the information?
Once you have completed the assessment to your satisfaction and analyzed the implications of the information you've collected, it's time to move on to the next phase of the planning process.

Step 2 – Accomplishments

It's never enough just to complete the assessment. If the assessment has been honest, it will undoubtedly point to specific needs in the community that can be addressed through the Community Experience Planning process.

What do we want to accomplish?

The temptation for many committees is to rush to solutions without thinking about what those solutions are supposed to accomplish. The purpose of the assessment process is to identify the gaps that must be filled. Whatever you perceive the needs to be in your community, now is the time to think about what you would like your community to be in the future.

Most planning processes begin with establishing or reviewing the mission for a specific organization. When dealing with multiple organizations or entities, each with its own mission statement, the more productive approach is to establish a common vision. Remember that you are going to try to honor everyone's mission statement to the greatest extent possible, even though some of those missions may be in opposition with each other. Ultimately, what does a healthy, holistic community look like to your steering committee? The process facilitator will help work through a discussion of the components that define your vision of success.

Once you have agreement on a vision statement, think about what it takes to support that vision. What are the core values that provide the parameters for obtaining that vision? There is no "right" number of core values, but a good rule of thumb is not to create so many that they become restrictive or hard to remember. Some communities encourage businesses and tourism venues to post the community vision and core values within public view, alongside the individual mission and core values of that location so that there is a visual link between the business or attraction and the overall community.

Remember that core values could become the key indicators on a sustainability "grade card" for your community as you monitor progress in the future.

Photo Essay

Whitehall, Montana, is a rural community of 1,200 near the Tobacco Root Mountains in Jefferson County. Lying along the famed route of Lewis and Clark's voyage of discovery to find the northwest passage, the community commissioned commemorative murals before and during the 2004-2006 Lewis & Clark Bicentennial. It helps tell their local history and slows down travelers for a longer look.

Lewis wrote: she was "our only dependence for a negociation with the Snake (Shoshoni) Indians on whom we depend for horses to assist us in our portage from the Missouri to the columbia river"

Prior to 1800, the Shoshoni had hunted buffalo in the Missouri River country. Escalating wars with the Blackfeet and Minnetaree tribes forced the Shoshoni to retreat to the mountains and valleys of Western Montana and Eastern Idaho where the expedition finally found Sacajawea's people.

When the Lewis and Clark Expedition reached the Three Forks of Missouri and started up the Jefferson River Valley, Sacajawea had returned to familiar country from her childhood.

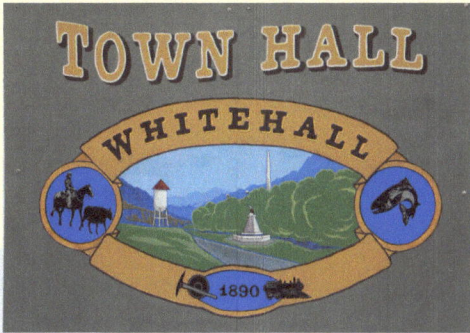

Semai Communities

MALAYSIA

The Semai people in the highlands of Malaysia once sold the local bird-winged butterflies and Rafflesia buds for pennies. The Malaysian Nature Society began working with the Ulu Geroh community of Semai people early in this new millennium to develop ecotours at the village that would provide income and jobs while protecting the unique flora and fauna of this rainforest region.

Rafflesia is the largest flower in the world with blooms more than a meter in diameter, but it involves a strenuous hike to see one in nature. The flower buds sell as curiosities in stores with no context for the unique mountain forest in which they grow. Their forest environment includes tree snakes that glide from tree to tree, giant insects such as 30-centimeter walking sticks, and buttressed ficus trees that create a high canopy. Selling off the prettiest butterflies and flowers was not a sustainable practice and gave little as compensation to the community for their efforts.

Ecotours bring people from all over the world who travel through Kuala Lumpur, a very modern capital city just two hours away by good roads. Semai people live in small communities in the forest and represent one of the

Paul Caputo

Indigenous Semai guides lead tourists along rainforest trails to find the unique rafflesia flower.

eighteen remaining tribes of Orang Asli people in Malaysia. In the past they were enslaved by Batak and Malay neighbors, hunted down by soldiers during a civil war and placed on reserves by the government. It was only in 2000 when they were officially recognized as human beings.

These indigenous forest people have an intimate knowledge of nature that is wonderful to experience on a visit to the village. They feed their guests fish caught in the local stream cooked and served with foraged fern leaves. They teach guests how to weave local reeds into traditional items and how to cast a purse net in the river to gather fish for the next meal. They give lessons on shooting a blowgun dart at a target and tell how they once used it to secure food in the forest. Local guides bring visitors into their homes to meet their families and share food. A village visit often concludes with an evening of traditional dance that brings the guests out with local people to try the steps and create rhythms with bamboo tubes. It is an engaging connection to the culture of the Semai and their strong conservation message about protecting the forest.

Semai meals are traditionally prepared using bamboo tubes heated in the coals of an open fire.

Raman demonstrates how a Semai nose flute is used to play traditional songs.

We enjoyed a visit with the people of Ulu Geroh and a few days later stopped in Gombak, another Semai community, to meet Raman and his family. He is a heritage interpreter, artist and musician who shares his culture at local hotels and invites people into his home to learn more about Semai food culture and craftsmanship.

The meal we enjoyed was prepared entirely in the hollow cavities of sections of green bamboo. Even the tea-water was boiled in an open fire in bamboo. Local fish, ferns and tapioca root were very tasty. As we ate, Raman told stories about his people's art and culture. He and his cousin Bahdua taught us how to make a nose flute and two-string guitar with bamboo and then performed traditional tunes with them. They also shared the craft of making blowguns from the internodes of a kind of bamboo unique to the Malaysian highlands.

As we prepared to leave their home, Raman invited us to purchase any of the items we had seen made or crafted by them previously. We had passed up similar items at the more commercial sales outlets, but made a significant number of purchases directly from the craftsman who demonstrated and connected us to the work first-hand.

—Tim Merriman

Writing a Vision Statement

Your vision summarizes what you want the future to look like. It can be an internal vision (what you hope your community will be) or an external vision (what you hope the world will look like if your community is successful) or it can express both sentiments. The main thing to remember is that your community leaders must all share the same vision or you will have limited chance of success in achieving it. Here are some examples of vision statements:

- Urban and diverse youth are empowered to protect our ocean and natural environment, improve the health of our communities, and strengthen the quality of life in our world. (external vision)

- We are the national leaders in workforce development. (internal vision)

Now, try writing one of your own. If you are working with a group, try starting with a listing of key words that might describe future conditions.

Key words:

Our vision:

Establishing Core Values

Core values express your beliefs about your community. For example, a core value might be that the community maintains or encourages environmentally sustainable practices among business and home owners. If that is a core value, then it means the community should provide information, opportunities, incentives, and rewards for creating, maintaining and improving environmental sustainability within the community.

Identify three or more values that are important to your community (single words, short phrases, or sentences will do – for example, "family" or "families need places to live, work, and play together"):

As you develop objectives for your community, use the core values to help guide how you approach what you want to accomplish.

What does our logic model look like?

Now that you know the common vision and core values, the next step is to determine how to achieve the results that will make that vision a reality. This is where the logic model begins to take shape. First, define the long-term goal(s) that will help in working toward the vision. Although it is tempting to jump next to outputs (what the community will provide) and then try to figure out why providing those outputs would be a good thing, it's in your best interest to think backwards here. Start by asking what, ultimately, you're trying to achieve. What benefits or positive impacts are desirable to help move you closer to the expressed vision? As in every step of this process, there is no single number of impact objectives that will be appropriate. You have to decide what level of challenge is a reasonable commitment for you and your partners.

Once the measurable impact objectives have been established, think about the outcome objectives. What actions will be necessary on the part of residents or visitors to help achieve the impact objectives? Like all objectives, outcomes should be specific and measurable so that they provide both a planning tool and an evaluation measure. Remember that it may take several outcomes to achieve one impact.

After looking at the outcomes that will be required to achieve the impacts, it's time to decide what outputs will be necessary to achieve the outcomes. This is the point at which you can let your creativity fly to think about the various programs, activities, media, facilities, and infrastructure that will support your vision by encouraging the actions you have identified in your outcome objectives. Of course, outputs must be considered within the bounds of the finances, staff, and other physical realities of the partners involved. If a particular output seems out of reach due to limited resources, the plan should include some way to close that gap – can volunteers be drafted to manage a special event? Or can grant money fund a start-up position? Will sponsors be available to help fund signs or other media? Although you may choose to leave your output objectives as vague as "create four experience packages," the details of what comprise each package will be needed to move to the next step of taking action.

Impact Objectives

Like all objectives, impact objectives should be specific and measurable. They represent the ultimate benefit(s) you hope to achieve for your community. Examples of impact objectives would be:

1. 100,000 acres of open space in the community will be protected from development within five years.

2. 80 percent of high school graduates will be college-bound each year.

3. Our community will be ranked in the top five destinations for the state on four major websites.

Can you find the specific and measurable components in the examples?

Now, think about your community project. What is the ultimate benefit you hope to achieve? Is there more than one? Write one or more objectives to express the impact you hope to have:

Look at the objective(s) you've written – can you find the measurable components? Measurability is important because it helps you determine if you have achieved success.

Outcome Objectives

Outcome objectives measure changes in behavior that are needed to achieve the impact objective. Examples of outcome objectives might be:

1. 20 families annually will participate in workshops on conservation easement opportunities.

2. 75 percent of middle school children will regularly participate in after-school community programs.

3. Five local attractions will collaborate in creating community experience packages.

Remember that it may take many outcomes to achieve just one impact. Now, think about your impact objective (or one of them). What types of behaviors will have to occur to achieve the positive impact or benefit that you hope to see? Write one or more outcome objectives that might be needed to achieve your impact objectives.

Circle the measurable factors to ensure that you're keeping your objectives specific enough to be useful in measuring effectiveness. Remember to only include measurements that you are willing to follow through on.

Output Objectives

The things that you do to influence behavior change can be expressed as output objectives. Just as it may take several outcomes to achieve one impact, it can take many outputs to achieve one outcome. Some outputs will help to accomplish more than one outcome. Examples of output objectives might be:

1. Develop community conservation workshops four times a year.

2. Develop after-school programs at all middle schools that encourage scholarship.

3. Invite community attractions to monthly partner planning meetings.

Pick one of your outcome objectives and write one or more output objectives that will help accomplish the desired behavior change. Take another look at your outcome objectives. Will any of the outputs you've suggested work for more than one outcome?

Use your output objectives to help create an action plan so that you know where to start in accomplishing your community project.

Remember that these work boxes are for practice only. You will need to create as many impact objectives, outcome objectives, and output objectives as are appropriate for your project. There is no set number of any of these levels that will guarantee success. It is your ability to write good objectives and then follow your own directions that will ensure great results.

Theme – Your Message Matters

When you think about your community, what is the one thing that you really want people to understand about it? Your theme is a message about what matters to the people who live there and who visit there. If the central message about your community isn't readily apparent, try listing a dozen or so of the important stories that should be told about the community.

Now look for common threads – can you group any of these stories into what might be considered subthemes? Try to use only two to four subthemes by writing a sentence that expresses the idea that ties that the group of stories together.

What is our central theme?

During the assessment step, you looked at whether any identifiable theme already exists. If not, you began to list the stories that make your community unique. By matching the stories against your core values, a central theme may begin to emerge. If it is not readily apparent, an interpretive planner can provide help with this step. Ideally, your central theme statement will be a single, simple sentence that expresses an idea or message about your community. Good themes are more than statements of simple fact – they should also contain a point of view or perspective that helps answer why that fact matters to anyone. A great theme statement will connect tangible things to intangible ideas. The best themes also include universal concepts that help all people understand and appreciate the expressed idea.

Theme statements may be used as or become the basis for promotional slogans, but beware of the marketing department that comes up with its own "theme" without being part of the overall planning process. There are many documented cases of communities and interpretive sites that have sent contradictory messages because the marketing department did not fully understand the ramifications of the core values expressed by the planning committee. For that reason, it is critical that the planning committee include the individual or individuals who will be responsible for promotions once the planning process is complete.

How do we define our experience packages to accomplish our objectives?

Defining an experience package can be done in any number of ways. After establishing the theme and subthemes (messages) to be communicated, you may want to make a matrix that defines audiences on one axis and the messages on the other axis. In the boxes on the matrix, you can identify specific outputs that might be appropriate for communicating messages to audiences. Or you might want to look at establishing experience packages by grouping activities and venues that appeal to a specific interest (for instance, a tour of all art galleries packaged with an art museum). Along the Billy the Kid Scenic Byway in New Mexico, experiences are packaged using a matrix of time and interest – here's the things to do if you have two hours and an interest in horses or here's the things to do if you have two days and an interest in cowboy history.

Now look for the big idea that communicates the importance of the subthemes and write a sentence that will tell people what matters most about this community.

Examples

1. Fort Collins: Where Renewal is a Way of Life

2. Damariscotta: Protecting the Down Home Feeling of Coastal Maine

3. Hangzhou: Our Past, Present, and Future Hinge on a Harmonious Relationship with Nature

There is no limit to the number of storylines you might ultimately express in a variety of ways throughout the community, but keeping to a thematic structure will help ensure that the main message isn't lost amidst a sea of individual facts or disparate stories. It may also help you define an architectural style or develop a marketing slogan.

national scenic byways program

Billy the Kid Scenic Byway Visitor Center offers visitors and residents the chance to match time with interest to develop an individualized Community Experience Package.

Using a large map and colored post-it notes is a good way to work with putting together experience packages. By placing color-coded notes on various locations on the map, it helps to reveal the physical relationships that connect the various subthemes and stories and identify any infrastructure needs that might be necessary to facilitate participation in those experiences.

How do we ensure everyone is working toward the same goal(s)?
Keeping the committee engaged in the planning process and checking in at regular points along the way to ensure that everyone is still on board with decisions that have been made helps to keep the process moving smoothly and towards that common vision. There will be times when someone's individual interest attempts to override the desires of the larger group. There are no easy answers for dealing with this situation, but your facilitator and committee chair are the ones to ensure that everyone's voice is heard and that consensus is reached before moving forward with various decisions. Consensus does not mean that everyone will get exactly what they want, but each partner

125

must agree that they intend to work toward the greater good before becoming involved with the process. Clearly stating vision, core values, goals, objectives, and message and keeping all of those elements in the forefront are key to achieving success. Civic engagement must include regular reporting of activities and decisions of the steering committee to ensure support for implementation, but true civic engagement means more than just reporting. It requires that the community be fully involved in the process. Once the plan reaches this stage, it's time for action.

Step 3 – Action

You've come a long way in your thought process at this point. Don't let the plan sit on the shelf. To effect positive change in your community, you must take action and implement the plans you've made.

Who needs to do what when?

An action plan identifies who is responsible for the outputs identified in the previous step and sets a schedule for implementation. It may be necessary to break the outputs down into specific action items at this point and depending on the number of outputs, the number of action items may seem overwhelming. The easiest way to do this is to create a chart with the specific output as the heading with columns below for action item, person responsible, date by which the item must be accomplished, and any resources that may be necessary to accomplish that item.

It may be advisable to tackle each output as a separate chart to hand directly to the partner(s) who are responsible for that particular output, since not everyone will be involved with every output. This keeps the number of action items from becoming discouraging. The steering committee chair can then maintain the collection of output charts so that there is someone who can keep a handle on the big picture and ensure that progress is being made.

How do we test our ideas before committing to action?

Before turning your committee loose on completing action items, it's a good idea to do a reality check to ensure that your ideas are sound. The first filter should include available budget and staff resources to manage and maintain whatever has been planned. Some communities identify a need for signage and put signs in place without first determining who will ultimately be responsible for upkeep. With no one agency or organization designated for that task, the signs fall into disrepair and begin to impinge on the quality of the experience. One scenic byway was ready to go forward with planning a visitor center that would require a staff of eight to run with no real way to pay that staff or get reliable volunteers. On testing the idea, they opted to go with a roadside information kiosk instead, saving a substantial sum of money in the process.

The theme and subthemes should be tested by focus groups to determine whether the messages being sent are the same ones being received. In the 1990s, the National Park Service commissioned a messaging study to determine what messages park superintendents believed they were sending. When they tested the public to determine what messages were being received, there was little to no overlap. Testing can help identify if there are problems with the assumptions you've made during the planning process, before money gets spent on implementation.

Developing a Community Grade Card
Planning and implementation are only the beginning for community stakeholders who aspire to build a stronger community identity grounded in their natural and cultural heritage. Once the action plan has been fully implemented, it's not enough to sit back and enjoy immediate results. Instead, ask yourself how and how often will you evaluate success in the future? What will let everyone involved enjoy a celebration when progress is made and reshape tactics when they are not? How will you monitor and report the long-term health of your community's heartbeat?

Sustainable Seattle created a set of sustainability indicators with specific targets for social, environmental and economic strategies that started with some realistic documentation of where the community was in each given area. These are long-term indicators that can be monitored on a regular basis to determine whether the community is improving, deteriorating, or holding its own. Grades or indicators turn vague hopes for meaningful change into a way that leaders can report on success or failure so that they can continually tweak the planned tactics and strategies to achieve objectives as time goes by.

Key stakeholders have to decide what the community grade card will measure and how often they will monitor progress. You must measure things that are reasonable to check on a regular basis and report them in a place where all can see such as the community's website, newspaper, cable TV, local café, or meeting locations. It is also important to do it on a regular schedule so all know when the progress report will be made. Some areas you wish to influence may take many years to show the progress you want. Some may stubbornly not seem to change or even worsen with your efforts. If monitoring becomes part of the community culture, it can help community members understand their role in keeping the community healthy and reveal specific problem areas before they become problems too big to solve.

What follow-up is required?
Even after the plan has been fully implemented, the work does not stop. If you want great word of mouth commentary on your community efforts, people must have great experiences in every way. The attitude and behavior of local people, especially those in the service industries, influence how residents and visitors perceive your community. Consistent training and the encouragement of continuing professional development throughout the community can make the difference.

National Association for Interpretation offers a Certified Interpretive Host training course and credential that takes about 16 hours to earn. The course is about one-third customer service and two-thirds informal interpretation. Informal interpretation simply uses a conversational approach to help an individual or group make an emotional connection with local resources. Anyone who meets and greets people can make a difference in helping people connect. A waitress, cashier, security person, receptionist or maintenance worker can ask questions, assess the person's interests, and make suggestions that may turn a routine visit into a rich and special experience.

Finally, the objectives you have established will serve as evaluation tools to test whether you have truly achieved what you set out to accomplish. As you write those impact objectives, think about a time frame that seems reasonable. When you are halfway to the established deadline, you may want to evaluate your effectiveness and then tweak anything that does not seem to be performing as expected. As you reach the deadline, evaluate again to see where you stand. If you have done a thoughtful job of planning and executing your ideas, your vision of a community with HEART should be a reality.

8 Resources for Staying HEART Healthy

Everyone can use a little help along the way. The following resources are provided as tools that might be useful as you begin your Community Experience Planning process.

Books

Brochu, Lisa. 2003. *Interpretive Planning: The 5-M Model for Successful Planning Projects*. Fort Collins, Colorado: InterpPress.

Brochu, Lisa, and Tim Merriman, Ph.D. 2008. *Personal Interpretation: Connecting Your Audience to Heritage Resources*. Fort Collins, CO: InterpPress.

Gilmore, James H., and B. Joseph Pine III. 2002. *The Experience Economy*. Boston, Massachusetts: Harvard Business School Press.

Gilmore, James H., and B. Joseph Pine III. 2007. *Authenticity: What Consumers Really Want*. Boston, Massachusetts: Harvard Business School Press.

Loewen, James, 1999. *Lies Across America: What Our Historic Sites Get Wrong*. New York City, New York: Touchstone.

Navone, John. March 8, 1994. "The Geography of Nowhere Has a Chianti Counterpoint." *International Herald Tribune.*

Shilling, Dan. 2008. *Civic Tourism: The Poetry and Politics of Place.* Prescott, Arizona: Sharlot Hall Museum Press.

HEART Workshops and Seminars

The authors and their HEART team leaders provide a variety of opportunities to learn more about putting the HEART into your community.

- Keynote presentations for your community or organization function
- Half-day seminar with instructional activities for creating your own Community Experience Plan
- Full-day HEART assessment for your community
- 3-day community interaction workshop to clarify your community's core values, logic model, and theme
- Custom consulting and facilitation in your community

Contact the authors by email at lisa@heartfeltassociates.com or tim@heartfeltassociates.com for more information.